ON THE

PRACTICABILITY OF AN INVASION

OF

BRITISH INDIA.

ON THE

PRACTICABILITY OF AN INVASION

OF

BRITISH INDIA;

AND ON THE

COMMERCIAL AND FINANCIAL PROSPECTS AND RESOURCES

OF

THE EMPIRE.

BY LIEUT.-COLONEL DE LACY EVANS.

GYAN

Published by

Gyan Publishing House
5, Ansari Road
Daryaganj, New Delhi-110002
Phone: 011-47034999, 9811692060
E-mail: books@gyanbooks.com

Distribution Network
gyanbooks.com
India, USA, Canada, UK, Australia, France

ISBN: 978-81-212-7783-9 (PB)
First Published, 1829

2nd Impression 2023

Printed at: Gyan Press, Delhi.

ON THE PRACTICABILITY OF AN INVASION OF BRITISH INDIA
Author: DE LACY EVANS

ON THE

PRACTICABILITY OF AN INVASION

OF

BRITISH INDIA.

ON THE

PRACTICABILITY OF AN INVASION

OF

BRITISH INDIA;

AND ON THE

COMMERCIAL AND FINANCIAL PROSPECTS AND RESOURCES

OF

THE EMPIRE.

" If we possessed Khiva, of which the conquest would not be difficult, ... *then would all the treasures of Asia enrich our country*, and WE should see realized the brilliant project of Peter the Great: *Masters of Khiva, many other States would be brought under our dependence.* In a word, Khiva is at this moment an advanced post, which . . . . would become the point of re-union for all the commerce of Asia, and WOULD SHAKE TO THE CENTRE OF INDIA, THE ENORMOUS COMMERCIAL SUPERIORITY OF THE DOMINATORS OF THE SEA." —*Colonel Mauravief, Russian Envoy to Khiva*—1826.

BY LIEUT.-COLONEL DE LACY EVANS.

LONDON:
PRINTED FOR J. M. RICHARDSON, CORNHILL.

MDCCCXXIX

THE *chief part of the following pages were drawn up before the passage of the Balkan by the Russian Army. The whole of the Essay (with the exception of these lines) was printed some time back, but the publication, through some circumstance, was withheld—unintentionally on the part of the writer, who was at the moment absent from town. Intermediately, a treaty of peace has been announced, which induces the prefixing of this notice.*

At such a time, it may not be extraneous to look back, for a moment, on the transactions of the four years' eventful reign of the present Czar, Nicholas.

At his accession, an insurrection took place, the importance of which was much magnified. The strength of it appears to have chiefly consisted in what must have totally hindered its ultimate success—namely, the loyalty of some regiments to the rightful heir of Alexander. Some thought in this country, that if the Autocrat had been then cut off, the greatness of the Empire had been put a stop to. But how soon are recent events forgotten! During the last hundred years alone about eight members of the Imperial Russian family have perished by poison, in dungeons, or by assassination. Amongst them was even the father of the reigning sovereign. Twice also during that period has the dynasty been violently changed in favour of foreigners, and even of women—one originally a peasant girl, the other a petty German princess. And in what respect did these catastrophes defeat the aggressive policy or avert the ambitious progress of the Muscovite state? Counting downward from Cæsar or Anthony for 500 *years, what a multitude of those who wore the purple, or of scions of the stock, may we not enumerate, that were slain by conspirators, or put aside in a like manner, without freeing the world from Roman bondage! And yet Rome was all that time in the decrepitude of its age, and, with little intermission, in a declining, distracted, and anarchical condition. How different from the rude, youthful, and ascending vigour of the present northern power!*

No sooner was the crown steadily placed upon the head of Nicholas, than his ambassador at the Porte gave in a peremptory ultimatum. The cantonments on the Prudthe were concentrated; the troops were assembled; six weeks were granted for a decision; at the expiration of which, if the demands should not be acceded to, the Principalities, it was announced, would be taken possession of. The Convention of Akerman followed, which was, in fact, an engraftment of a new and galling treaty upon that of Bucharest. The Turks openly confessed that they yielded, with " the knife to their throats."

This done, Persia is turned upon; and a province, which covers the capital, and comprises, by its features, the absolute key on that side of the Shah's dominions, are wrested from him, under pretences of the most monstrous and glaring futility.

The Royal Family of Persia being now lost in public estimation, are at present actually kept upon the throne of that country, through the good pleasure of the Cabinet of St. Petersburgh, for such purposes as, no doubt, will, in due season, be developed.

Not a moment is then lost in recommencing operations of a decisive character against the Porte. The proceedings in Greece being intermediately in progress, a President is actually furnished to it from the foreign office of the Emperor.

It is almost idle to talk of the particular terms of the treaty of Adrianople. The general consequence of these transactions is—that one of the States, hitherto comprehended in the European Confederacy, and most important by its geographical position, has virtually ceased to exist.

Such has been the busy and triumphant course of this judicious and able prince;—whose moderation has been so ridiculously a theme of admiration, and who, in reality, has already achieved more for the substantial aggrandisement of his power, at the very outset of his career, than have the greater part of his most successful predecessors in a whole reign.

The situation of the British Representatives at Constantinople and Petersburgh has, during the two campaigns just passed, been any thing but an enviable one. They have had to contend with the pen against the sword,—which is rarely an equal contest. The overthrow of the Ottoman power in Europe has been so utter and irremediable, and the dismemberment so vast, that it may now be well doubted whether the Sultan has been wisely counselled, in yielding the sanction of a recognition to the respite,—for it is no peace,—which records in a formal manner his subjugation. The shadow of a resistance could only be offered; but it may be conjectured, that it should have been offered. The ferocious Sultan, if indisposed to play in reality the part of a soldier, should perhaps have retired into Asia, and left to his Lieutenants the task of carrying on, if possible, for a little longer, the contest on this side of the Bosphorus. Henceforth, at all events, he cannot be a free agent on the banks of that channel. The sooner he is compelled by the neutral powers to remove the seat of his ostensible government to Smyrna or some other place in that part of his remaining territory, the better for himself and for other states. It will now probably be the object of the Russians to keep him where he is, to call him an ally, and to make use of him so long as it shall prove convenient to do so. This is a sort of game which our own government in India has played over and over again.

We have there at present crowds of native Princes who are no longer of any utility it is true, but who have become so innoxious, that their pageantry and large incomes are still granted to them.

By the rumoured stipulations of this Treaty, a sum equal to about 150 *millions sterling, compared with our income, is required from the Sultan, whose resources are totally exhausted, and who could not obtain credit for a stiver. Hopes are entertained that some modification may be procured on this head. It will not much signify. Four fortresses on the Danube are to be demolished; four other fortresses in Asia, with the fertile and beautiful Pashalic of Akhalzik, are to be ceded; the greater part of European Turkey is to remain under the guardianship of the Czar; and the intention is avowed by one of the supposed articles, of placing the commerce of the Euxine, Asoph, Marmora, and even that of the port of Constantinople, at the disposal of Russia! That of the Caspian is already so; that of all the Levant would of course be soon similarly influenced.*

12th October.

INTRODUCTORY OBSERVATIONS.

Lord Clive, Mr. Warren Hastings, and the Marquess Wellesley, are the names most prominent in the annals of the British affairs in India. To the elevated capacity and courage of these individuals, rather than to any great scheme of original ambition premeditated by governments, our supremacy in the East is attributable.

There is only left to the men of the present times the easier task of preserving this achievement, and of deriving from it such advantages as it may be susceptible of yielding.

To the last named of the above historic characters,

The Marquess Wellesley,

the following pages are inscribed, as being the Statesman now living who will best know whether they contain anything worthy of attention; and because he cannot but feel a deep interest in whatever may involve the security of possessions, with the acquisition of which his own fame is so mainly associated.

I.

With reference to that part of what follows, which may be considered in the light of an exposition of evidence or authorities, it will be sufficient to remind the reader, that the question at issue comprehends matters of no ordinary consequence: amongst which may be enumerated the safe and unimpaired retention of a source of from 20 to 25,000,000*l*. of revenue, the whole of which is at the disposal of, and a large part of which might unquestionably, if emergency arose, be employed by, the Government of the superior State for its relief or necessities generally.

Further, that this dependency includes what, for our manufactural produce, we stand so eminently in need of—viz. about 100,000,000 * of consumers, whose means of consumption are, under the influence of tranquillity and a stable authority, rapidly increasing; and our unfettered

---

* Malte Brun gives a detailed statement of the population, the result of which is—83,000,000 for the British territory; for British tributary, subsidiary, and protected allies, 40,000,000: total, 123,000,000.

admission to whose markets no more depends on the caprice, policy, or power, as in other cases, of a foreign potentate, than it is liable to prohibitory tax or impediment of any sort, beyond such as we may ourselves be pleased to dictate or judge expedient.

II.

By official statements lately published*, the whole numerical strength of the Russian army, for the year 1818, amounted to 1,000,000, (comprising, however, no doubt, all the establishments connected with it, as well as several local and stationary corps.) Between 1818 and 1825, a reduction is stated to have been effected, in the proportion of one-third, which may therefore be estimated at 330,000 men. From 1825 to the present time augmentations have been taking place, and the army is probably by this time again raised to at least the same strength at which it was in 1818.

We may therefore calculate the expenditure for the army of 1818 as equal to that of the present year, exclusive of war charges. The amount stated

* *Weydemer.*

is 6,000,000*l.* sterling * for the military; and, for the naval department (comprising † twenty-five line-of-battle ships and as many frigates), a fraction under 1,000,000*l.* sterling. The expenditure under this latter head is now probably double what it was.

In the same year (1818) our army amounted (vide Parliamentary Returns) to 113,000 men; and the charge on account of it (including ordnance and militia) to 11,500,000*l.*

In the French Budget for the present year we find that an army of nearly 250,000 men, or (adding the different establishments similar to those which are probably included in the Russian statement) say 300,000 men, costs 190,000,000 of francs, or about 8,000,000*l.* sterling.

If these statements approximate the truth, Russia can maintain, within her own frontiers, nearly three times as many troops as France can, for the same money. The disparity of expense being in a still greater ratio, with reference to

---

* "Aucune armée de l'Europe, proportion gardée en nombre, n'est entretenue à moins de frais que l'armée russe. Son entretien, en 1818, se montoit à 150,000,000 roubles, Comme elle se trouve maintenant (1825) diminuée au moins d'un tiers, les dépenses sont proportionnellement reduites. L'entretien de la flotte se monte à 24,000,000." —*Weydemer.*

† "6000 cannons, 80,000 marins, de tout grade."—*Ibid.*

English troops. The only drawback in favour, on this point, of the resources of England and France, being the probably superior completeness of organization to which their military establishments have arrived, and from which a greater proportion of relative efficiency in the field must be a consequence.

The national debt of Russia being under 55,000,000*l.* sterling, it will absorb an interest of about 3,000,000*l.* per annum. The yearly interest of debt with which the resources of France are burdened, reaches, I believe, at present, to about 12,000,000*l.* sterling.

The pay of the servants of the Russian Government, of all grades, both civil, naval, or military, is known to be extremely small—smaller even *

* Admission to the public service of Russia is, in one respect, a boon conferred by the government, and therefore a reason for reducing the pecuniary remuneration or pay: the officer is substantially raised in the scale of society, and so is the private to a respected condition, exchanging at the same time the discipline of the camp for the knoot, the caprice, or the irresponsible violence of a master. Besides, it is easier to content the serf, from the hard and perhaps stinted life he has previously endured. Such a subsistence must be tendered to the English peasant or artisan as will induce him to surrender his personal freedom, and submit to the chance of corporal punishment.

than the proportionate value of money would lead to the inference of. This may, probably, in many cases, be a vicious system, leading to peculation and the worst irregularities. It may be injurious to the resources of the State generally, but it clearly makes the actual sum in the treasury go further, or count for more, than it otherwise would do, for the time being.

It is, perhaps, almost impossible to ascertain, with exactitude, the value of money in Russia and its *bordering* states, compared with that assignable to it in England or France. It is obvious, however, that six millions sterling would fall wonderfully short of maintaining or retaining, in any way, the services of one million of persons, of any description, in either of the two latter countries.

There is, of course, an ultimate limit to the resources of every country, be the industry, ingenuity, and talent of its inhabitants what they may. And it is equally clear that England and France have already arrived (so far as relates to their internal resources) much nearer to that *extreme limit* than Russia has done.

The latter country has immense natural resources, whose existence, so far from approaching any period of exhaustion, have been little more than ascertained. In its present state, its produce considerably exceeds* its consumption; and it wants nothing but greater freedom of exertion, and an adequate vent for its commodities in the interior parts of the country (and particularly to the southward), to occasion an increase of population and of means, astonishingly rapid.† These additional vents which she requires, her government seems by no means remiss in its efforts to procure—so far, at least, as the opening of new roads, the construction of canals, encouragements to commercial enterprise; to which may well be added, its declared determination of at length securing an uninterrupted passage into the Mediterranean.

It is true that the increased wealth of the Czar's dominions would enable their vast population to purchase a larger quantity than hitherto of our wrought goods. But, were this calculation to sway us in any considerable affair of international policy, we should manifestly proceed on a very insecure presumption, or rather on a lamentable fallacy; inasmuch as, although the

---

* The annual excess of grain 1802, 1803, 1804, was calculated (by official returns) at from 84 to 120,000,000 of bushels. An extreme abundance commences at Kasan; at Astrakan and Orenberg the surplus agricultural produce is also remarkable.

† Malthus.

internal condition of Russia has been already decidedly undergoing a great and accelerated improvement, still our *export* trade thither has in no respect kept pace with this amelioration, but, on the contrary, has been either stationary or even actually receding in value; the present estimate of which being no more than about two millions sterling.

And the reason of this is no less obvious. The Russian government seems to regard it as best for the promotion of its own industry and manufactures, to exclude, as far as it well can do, the competition with *ours*, by burdening the introduction of British goods with severe, and, in some instances, totally prohibitory duties, or even by direct enactments to that end. This is not, then, a matter of assumption. The autocratic government has, for some years back, been unequivocally announcing, by various unfriendly commercial regulations, the description of its rivalry; nay, an almost hostile animus, in reference to the produce of our industry.

Nor is it in the least improbable that political views form a large part of the motive of these fiscal obstructions. And if this be the case, so far from being justified in calculating on relaxations of them, and a return to a more favourable system, we should, with much greater reason, look to their being pushed to a far more irksome and injurious extent, in proportion to the increase of power in the government thus already betraying, in so marked a way, inimical feeling.

The same official returns, before quoted, estimate the revenue for 1825 at 450,000,000 of roubles (*en assignats*). This gives the sum of about eighteen millions and a half sterling, (valuing the rouble assignat at ten pence.) There will, therefore, (deducting interest on debt) be above *fifteen millions* sterling remaining as a surplus for the purposes of government.

The *surplus* revenue of France may at present, after a similar deduction, be about *twenty-five millions* sterling; that of England, about twenty-two millions.

Now, if we look to the price of grain, which is usually reckoned the best criterion of the relative value of money, we shall find that, from 1817 to 1824, the average of wheat in the Black Sea was 22*s*. 4*d*. per quarter. At Bourdeaux, and other grain-markets of France, it was from 37*s*. to 40*s*. or 41*s*. per quarter. While, for the same article, the last declared weekly "imperial average," which governs importation, was 66*s*. 7*d*.*

Now, if we deduct the 6*s*. 7*d*., as being about equivalent to the supposed inferiority of the

---

* See *London Gazette,* Friday, Sept. 1829.

wheat of the Euxine to that of England, we shall have this conclusion, that *twenty-two shillings* will procure as much of the chief necessary of life at *Odessa*, as *forty shillings* will in *France*, or as *sixty shillings* will in *England*.*

And if we make a further allowance on account of a higher price of wheat in other parts of Russia, averaging about 2*s*. per quarter, we shall still, probably, be obliged to admit this result, namely, that 15,000,000*l*. of disposable revenue in that empire or the adjacent countries, must be equivalent, according to the foregoing scale, to, at the least, 30,000,000*l*. or even 35,000,000*l*. in England.

If these data approach to correctness, the ambition of the Russian court can hardly be much embarrassed—as so many have supposed—through THE PENURY OF ITS EXCHEQUER!

To-day (22nd Sept.) there is an account in the papers of a Russian loan, of one million sterling, lately advertised for; and about three days back carried into the Amsterdam Exchange. In two hours, *five times the sum desired* was subscribed

---

* An equally probable criterion may perhaps be the *price of labour*. A labourer, for instance, in Poland, (which is not the cheapest country of Russia) receives 4½*d*. a day; his wages, counting other advantages, may be put at 6*d*. While, in England, the agricultural labourer is paid by his employer or the parish about 1*s*. 10*d*. or 2*s*. a day.

for, or offered!—A successful army never wants credit.

III.

A despondent way of thinking, in reference to our financial condition, is by no means new or peculiar to the present times. A very cursory glance at the popular writers or orators of the last century will shew the contrary.

About eighty years ago, the publication called the "*World*" was the principal, and almost the only work of that kind of the time. The reader may remember a paper in it, headed thus:—

"AN ANTIDOTE TO DESPONDENCY, *or progressive Assertions from respectable Authority, tending to prove, that the Nation was actually undone prior to the Revolution in* 1688; *and that it has remained in a continued state of Ruin or Decay ever since that memorable Era.*"

"It has often been remarked, that the English are more inclined than any other nation to view the dark side of the prospect—to fear every thing and to hope for nothing. In the month of November, in particular, the state suffers exceedingly; and whoever seriously sits down to consider, in that gloomy season of the year, the situation of the country, concludes, after mature reflection, *that the country is undone;* or that matters are so bad, that the business of government cannot possibly be carried through another session," &c.

About twenty years before that period, we may gather, from a similar publication, what the notion then was on the same topic:—" The *vast load* of debt, (says the *Craftsman*, 1736) under which the nation still *groans*, is the true source of all those *calamities and gloomy prospects* of which we have so much reason to complain."

From Torbuck's debates of the succeeding year (1737) the following is given, as from one of the parliamentary speakers of the time:—" For my part, I do not know any one necessary of life upon which we have not some tax or another, except water; and we can put no ingredient I know of into water, in order to make it palatable and cheerful, without paying a tax. We pay a tax for air, and for the light and heat of the sun in the day-time, by means of our tax upon windows; and for light and heat in the night time, by means of our duties upon coals and candles: we pay a tax upon bread, meat, roots, and herbs of all kinds, by means of our salt duty*; we pay a tax upon small-beer by means of the malt tax; and a heavy additional tax upon

* *Sinclair.*

strong beer by way of excise. Nay, we cannot have any clean thing to put upon our backs, either of woollen or linen, without paying a tax by means of the duty on soap," &c.

Lord Littleton, in 1774, thus speaks of the contrasted condition of *France and England*:—

"What are, then, the circumstances of this kingdom and of France? On one side, mortgaged revenues, credit sunk at home and abroad, an exhausted, dispirited, discontented people. On the other, *a rich and popular government*, strong in alliances, in reputation, in the confidence and affection of its subjects.—Our well-equipped fleets and well-dressed troops give, to be sure, an air of magnificence; but then it is well known *that we owe almost fifty millions*, and have been forced to apply the sinking fund, not to discharge that debt, *but to furnish out these shews*; whilst, in most parts of England, *gentlemen's rents are so ill-paid* *, and the weight of taxes lies so heavy upon them, that those who have nothing from the court can scarce support their families."

About twenty years after this doleful declamation, which then passed current as excellent logic, the *rich and popular* government his lordship alludes to—ceased to exist.

---

* *How like the present dreadful times!*

In 1761, Mr. Hume observes, "The first instance of a debt contracted upon parliamentary security, occurs in the reign of Henry VI. The commencement of this pernicious practice deserves to be noted ; a practice the more likely to become pernicious the more a nation advances in opulence (!) and credit. The ruinous effects of it are now become apparent, *and threaten the very existence of the nation.*"

Nor does this conviction of impending ruin, on the part of our great and acute historian, appear to have been hastily (if ever) relinquished, since, fifteen years afterwards, we find him still declaring his unabated persuasion of the same unfortunate issue—thus :—

"I suppose there is no mathematical, still less an arithmetical demonstration, that the road to the Holy Land was not the road to Paradise, as there is, that the endless increase of national debts is the direct road to national ruin. *But having now completely reached that goal,* it is needless at present to reflect on the past. It will be found in the present year, 1776, that all the revenues of this island, north of Trent and west of Reading, are mortgaged or anticipated for ever. Could the small remainder be in a worse condition were those provinces seized by Austria and Prussia? There is only this difference, that some event might happen in Europe which would oblige these great monarchs to disgorge their acquisitions. But no imagination can figure a situation which will induce our creditors to relinquish their claims, or the public to seize their revenues. So egregious, indeed, has been our folly, that we have even lost all title to compassion in the *numberless calamities that are waiting us*."

Notwithstanding all these *terrible mortgages*, *numberless calamities*, &c. &c., we subsequently scraped together a sufficient pecuniary residue to enable us to contend with or subsidize half Europe, and overthrow one of the most powerful military monarchies ever established. If any unlearned person, however, at that time, ventured to doubt the sagacity of these predictions, he would, perhaps, have been treated with some degree of contempt. I venture to hope, nevertheless, that the opinions of some of the great doctors of the present day may be looked upon, some forty or fifty years hence, with equal surprise.

After the American war, there seemed certainly much additional reason for sombre anticipations.—" If the premises are just (says Lord Stair, in a speech of his, 1783), or nearly just, and nothing effectual is done to prevent their consequences, the infallible, inevitable conclusion that follows is, *that the state is a bankrupt*, and that those who have trusted their *all* to the public faith, are in very imminent danger of becoming (*I die pronouncing it*) BEGGARS."

It is not with the remotest idea of making light of taxation and public burdens, or of pandering to the vices or prodigality of any government, that those well-known passages are here introduced, but merely to show, that *general opinion* does not always prove (*in the event*) to be infallible.

Now, it is quite positive that the two worst periods of depression, just referred to, were immeasurably more unpropitious, to all appearance, both financially and generally, foreign and domestic, than is our present condition,—I mean those which succeeded the American war, and the war of succession, 1715—1783.

Indecisive results in the field, and the disgraceful treaty of Utrecht, completely obscured the glory of the victories gained during the preceding contest. Discreditable as the result was, it is hard to find fault with those who wished to put an end to the war—for the people throughout *every* class were sinking into penury—there was, in those days, but little resource from commerce ; the public credit was deduced to a most embarrassing discount ; 6 and 6½ per cent. interest was paid on loans ; even as much as 15 per cent. was paid for an accommodation to the South Sea Company*; and the net revenue was under four millions and a half, from which there was to be deducted three millions and a quarter due on account of interest to the public creditor!

What was our condition in 1783?—We had lost character, both at home and abroad,—we had lost territory to an immense extent,—we had been unsuccessful on sea and land,—our wisdom and courage were both impugned,—the interest then payable on the debt had been swelled to 9,000,000, the revenue being no more than 12,000,000.

Instead of sinking, however, as so many apprehended, the nation rapidly rose to a height of financial and commercial wealth beyond what the most sanguine ever dared to anticipate; and I think it will not easily be proved that there is more, or anything near so much, reason, at the present crisis, to distrust the national fortunes, or to require the remotest acquiescence at our hands, tending to compromise any great principle or interest of the state.

But as the question of the real state of the national resources is one which intimately concerns the foreign policy of the country, I venture

* The bank had lent government 1,000,000 at 8 per cent.

to pursue a little further these preliminary remarks.

That distress prevails in several districts and amongst particular classes is but too true; but, if we can trace this unfortunate circumstance to sufficient, but partial, temporary, or remedial causes, we shall not be warranted in passing at once, without further inquiry, to a belief that the total *sum* of the national wealth is DIMINISHED OR DIMINISHING.

The inferior or poorer classes of the farmers, of the shop-keepers, and of the population of the manufacturing districts, appear to be the *chief* sufferers. But it is not, I am aware, confined to these: the pressure is communicated to other portions of society, from various sources. Working for foreign markets must, in its nature, be always a business liable to fluctuation. This must arise from the varying speculations of the capitalists, according to the greater or less saleableness of particular articles in the countries with which they correspond. This is an inherent drawback, not to be remedied by any legislature. But when the periods of depression and want of employ predominate, or are excessive, extraneous or more general causes must be presumed to be in operation.

Learned theories have been broached about the

superiority of commerce to agriculture,—of agriculture to commerce,—of the inutility of colonies, —of the sufficiency of internal industry and trade for every useful purpose,—of the impolicy of foreign alliances,—or of concerning ourselves with the affairs or quarrels of other nations, &c. &c. In short, our own markets, and the means of defending our own shores, being, it is insinuated, the only things requiring our attention. Such, at least, are inferences from the doctrines alluded to—doctrines which are not unfrequently recommended by respectable names, and with all the pomp and imposingness of scientific phraseology.

Nothing, however, is more clear (at least, as I should think, to common apprehension) than that a country of such moderate extent and ordinary intrinsic resource could never have arrived at the power and greatness which ours has done without many combined advantages; and, amongst these, especially, a flourishing agriculture, as well as a flourishing and extensive commerce, foreign and domestic. An extended commerce with very remote countries cannot be carried on with security, for any length of time, without conveniently situated sea-ports and depôt fortresses for our ships;—these cannot be defended without troops;—troops cause umbrage to the natives; —then follows, but too probably, the necessity of withdrawing those troops, or of subjugating, in self-defence, those who would expel them.—Conquest, if successful, is the result; which (if regulated by ordinary prudence) none but those who affect to be legislators, while they are better qualified to be behind counters, will be disposed to deem a political evil.

Commerce with countries nearer home should require only *unobstructed* admission to their markets; but political or commercial rivalry may, and does, occasion such obstructions. They were attempted on a great scale by Bonaparte in his Berlin and Milan Decrees, and in the wars which he waged with continental states to enforce them. To prevent the success of such attempts, *political influence* or *equality, if not ascendancy*, are requisite.

Other sources of the disproportionate power and political prosperity which this nation has enjoyed, are to be found in its *institutions* (which were better than those of surrounding states), and in its exemption for so many ages from hostile invasion. The security of these institutions must, in a large degree, be attributable to the sea, which surrounds us as a barrier of defence. But the sea would be no barrier without a triumphant fleet upon it; and a naval force derives its nourishment and *being* from a superior maritime commerce.

It was by acting upon this obvious chain of

consequences, by fostering industry both at home and abroad, and by defending the interests of both, in their boldest and widest comprehension, —through justice and spirit, and by the SWORD,— that the inhabitants of some unwholesome marshes near the estuary of the Rhine were enabled, during a glorious epoch, to rank themselves with the proudest and most ancient empires.

Not long after, they began to calculate after a more narrow fashion—something, it may be feared, in the manner of some of our own well-intentioned political arithmeticians. *Money* now became to be considered, not as an *accessary*, but as the sole *good*.

Presently, and almost within our own memory, this same people, whose private citizens, well-educated and patriotic merchants, and courageous burgomasters, deserved and possessed the estimation of nobles and princes—this same people, who, after throwing off the cruel yoke of Philip, contested with us the dominion of the sea,—who baffled the science of the implacable Alva, and victoriously repelled the armies of Louis,—were known to sell gunpowder to the Sans Culotte battalions, which came to besiege their towns, and avowedly to trample upon their necks.

Such is, of course, the fate reserved for others who would follow a similar system.

From the character of enlightened and munificent merchants, and no less of manly and sound politicians, the Dutch dwindled into a species of Israelitish peddlers, chiefly devoted to the careful hoarding of their pelf,—forgetting the way in which it was got, and by which alone it could be honourably secured*.

Transition, though for eventual good, brings partial or temporary evil.

1st. The restriction of cash-payment, during the war, has been the cause of a momentous reactionary measure.

2nd. Improvements, subsequent to that period,

---

* In 1815, when the great cause of national and European independence was again at stake, the Hollanders were cold and apathetic. They did not bring 20,000 men into the field. In the war of the succession, they had stipulated on equal terms, in money, troops, and ships, with England and the empire. In 1702, they furnished a military quota of 110,242 men, of which 79,858 were Dutch, the remainder Germans, in the pay of their High Mightinesses.

It is true, a native sovereign, a constitution, and a national existence, have been restored to them, but not, as before, the result of their own noble efforts, but chiefly of our generosity and policy. They are still great calculators, and a provident, money-getting, money-saving people. But the spirit, it is to be feared, has fled; and the first French or Prussian army which is in a condition to advance against their once well-defended frontiers, and is not withheld by other powers from doing so, will take away both their money and their liberty.

in machinery*, threw millions, for a short time, out of employ, or drove them to other occupations. The result of these improvements, added to the monopoly of maritime commerce, gave a new and prodigiously favourable impetus to the affairs of the country, and to the resources available for public use.

3rd. After a warfare on the largest scale, embracing all parts of the world, involving previously unheard of disbursements, there came, at the general peace, restricted expenditure, rivalry in maritime commerce, rivalry in manufactures.

4th. Having the fear of Bonaparte and democracy no longer before their eyes, the rich and

---

* The application of steam-power to carriages seems to be now very confidently counted on. Should this take place, the advantages, to *us*, in particular, would perhaps be scarcely less than accrued from the improvements above-mentioned. We have a greater number of horses, by many hundred thousands, employed in the conveyance of passengers through the interior of the country than any other people. I have heard it computed, that one million of horses are required for the use of the mail and stage coaches. Should these be rendered unnecessary, there would be food for an additional 3,000,000 of people at the public disposal. Two horses are said to consume as much of the produce of the land as seven human beings.

The statistician, *Adrien Balbi*, computes the horses in the United Kingdom at 1,900,000; in France, 2,500,000; in European Russia, 12,000,000.

influential compelled the ministry to forego the most productive, least burdensome, and (with all its defects) least inequitable of all the taxes—the income tax.* Thus, in fact, transferring their share of the public burdens to the shoulders of those not so well able to bear them, and on whose account they were *not* chiefly incurred.

5th. The law for restoring the currency to its previous value,—to the expediency or inexpediency of which these remarks do not refer,—the effècts as a *transition* (to which commercial communities are necessarily so much more exposed than any others) being all it is here attempted to enumerate. By this law, the *export merchant* (in some respects), the *manufacturer for foreign markets*, and the *Exchequer*, were partially benefited,—the latter, by the enhancement of revenue still remaining to it, after the compulsory loss of the tax above-mentioned. On the other hand, there also followed a change, to an enormous extent, in all *pre-existing* contracts, funded, leasehold, mortgage, &c. Perhaps, as much as *two or three thousand millions* worth of property must have been thus affected without

* If this tax had not been wrested from Ministers, and its operation had been rendered less objectionable, a very great diminution of the annual burdens of the country might have been by this time effected, without the painful consequences which other less productive ones have caused.

the possibility of readjusting agreements between the individuals throughout society mutually concerned. I am neither impugning nor commending, being neither disposed nor probably competent to do either, but merely throwing together what appear to me to be a few of the facts, a consideration of which may go to dispel some erroneous conclusions. But the chief drawback or anomaly inherent to this last measure was, that it actually conveyed over a gratuitous boon from the already most heavily burdened classes to those who had least title to the gift :—the annuitant, the fundholder or public creditor,* the mortgagee ;—all of whom were before actually in the possession of undue fiscal exemptions. This operated, in fact, as a vast transfer of property—one item of which had the effect of adding to the national debt what was equivalent to one or two hundred millions sterling. Those who suffer, of course loudly complain—the gainers are silent†.

---

* I believe that, according to the price of gold at the time, the average value of a pound-note during the war was 14*s.* 11*d.*—so that we are now paying about 20*s.* for every 14*s.* 11*d.* then contracted for.

† It is not a debt of eight hundred millions, as described in common parlance, that has been contracted, but the payment of an annuity of (at present) about twenty-eight millions. The *principal*, of eight hundred millions, being purely a nominal and variable value. The creditor cannot

Then, with respect to irregularity in the repartition of taxes;—let us take, for instance, the beer and malt tax of six or seven millions produce, almost the whole of which is paid by those in humble life; the gentleman of fortune, who brews in his own house, being nearly free from its operation: and then the curious monopoly with which it is saddled—injurious and obnoxious at once to the labourer who consumes the beverage, and to the landed proprietor, who grows the material from which it is extracted.

Then, with respect to the repartition of the poor-rate levy of seven or eight millions:—a parish, such, for instance, as that of St. Giles's, inhabited by the necessitous indigent, will have to pay, perhaps, four times as much in the pound as an adjoining one, St. James's,* consisting of

---

demand any principal. The Government may, at any time, redeem this annuity, according as the treasure in hand admits of their going into the market to buy stock, the purchase being made at the price of the day. And if the saleable value of the funds, now nearly ninety, fell to under fifty, as was the case at one period of the late wars, and it were then possible for the Government to send four hundred millions sterling into the market, the whole of what is called our debt of eight hundred millions might with that sum be bought up, or an investment of stock made, equivalent to it.

* Parish of St. James's, 1*s.* 2*d.* in the pound, poor-rate for 1829—St. Giles's, 3*s.* 10*d.*

the residences of the most affluent persons in the country. I happen to know a parish near the metropolis, the whole of which is the estate (and it is of great value) of one person. He farms it, and takes care to discharge his people after the eleventh month, to prevent a settlement. The consequence is, that the poor and populous parishes on either side have to pay a large part of the wages of his labourers. Then there is the army of lawyers, a good portion of whom are engaged in retarding or baffling justice, and in defeating the laws; and which portion of whom, at least, are unproductive recipients of the general means.* But these, and many others, are all REMEDIAL.

"*Notwithstanding* (says Mr. Ricardo) *the immense expenditure of the English government during the last twenty years, there can be little doubt but that the increased production, on the part of the people, has more than compensated for it. The national capital has not merely been unimpaired, it has been greatly increased, and the* ANNUAL REVENUE OF THE PEOPLE, EVEN AFTER THE

---

* I am not unaware of the splendid ability and worth comprised in the great profession of the law; but that is not enough to palliate abuses of such grievous extent. Other armies, beside those of the sword and long robe just mentioned, would also, no doubt, admit of reduction.

PAYMENT OF THEIR TAXES, IS PROBABLY GREATER AT THE PRESENT TIME THAN AT ANY FORMER PERIOD OF OUR HISTORY."

Still pauperism spreads, and demoralization with it. The evil, however, is not the diminution, but the inequality of wealth ;* and, unfortunately, the nature and repartition of the taxes, instead of tending to remedy, are calculated to promote, to aggravate most glaringly, this inequality. If means, however, are to be found, in one order of society, for alleviating any excessive pressure on another, we may be well assured that the present Government will fearlessly advance to effect that end.

But in estimating the relative financial strength of states, the question is *not* the *distribution*, but the AGGREGATE of available resource.

And that this has actually augmented, if from no other authority, we might safely contend, on the strength of the above extract.

But who, that has passed through the country with a mind disabused from the unscrupulous assertions of party, but must be convinced of the fact? Where are the appearances of decay or neglect—of an enfeebled or paralysed industry?

On the contrary, a vigilant and energetic care

* I believe Mr. Peel, in the last Session of Parliament, stated his conviction to the same effect.

is visible every where. Nothing seems to lie fallow. The divisions and subdivisions of proprietorship are strictly and tenaciously kept up. The fields wear the aspect of a garden. A considerable portion of the people are far better dressed than in former years, seek and possess more comforts, and are becoming more intelligent and educated. New roads are opening at great expense, the old ones are perfecting, shorter lines are devised.* If five hundred yards of distance can be saved, there seems to be no difficulty in procuring as many thousands wherewith to effect it. Well-appointed public carriages and magnificent horses follow in rapid succession along every line, with a dispatch indicating that the passengers stand much more in need of time than money.

In how many directions, also, may be seen commencing, or in process of completion, new canals, railways, superb bridges, and other public works—not usually of a perishable, cheap, or frail material, as would be the case were funds really deficient, but of durable iron and massive stone. Nor does utility alone seem

* Roads of the United Kingdom, 200,000 miles; internal navigation 2600 miles. It is calculated that, within the last half century, there have been laid out on roads, canals, rivers, docks, and sea-ports, about 100 millions sterling.

to be consulted. Many of these works are proofs of a triumphant science, as they are monuments of ornamental art, destined to embellish the country in which they have been reared, for many ages to come. Some—the Menai bridge, for instance, just completed, or the Waterloo—demanded (either of them) an expenditure equal to a whole year's surplus revenue of the empire in the reign of George the First or Queen Anne.

Observe the description of household furniture now in use. Is it not more choice, more frequently replaced by a new fashion, more curiously wrought and neatly finished, than formerly.

All branches of trade and commerce, and every town, seaport, or entrepôt, depending on particular branches of commerce, do not, it is true, equally flourish and thrive. But if some articles of produce have lost in value by desuetude or competition (foreign or domestic), others are in request which were not before invented or in being. Of the classes which have not thriven, in the degree of former times, are the West India proprietors. Many of these gentlemen purchased estates in England with the produce of the sugar-cane of insular America, and are now lords of the soil. Some of them derived, from the same source, twenty, forty, sixty thousand a year, during the war. Of course they went into Parliament—the great arena for the defence or acquisition of immunities; and were enabled to baffle or brave, for a long time, and do so still, the appeals of philanthropists, the remonstrances or frowns of ministers. Such immense profits could not be perpetual. Foreign colonies also produce sugar and molasses; the seas are once more the high road of nations; and the traffic in human beings, and the discipline of the whip, are somewhat restricted. But it is the augmented property of the mass of the nation which is here only contended for.*

Some of the greater country-houses of the ancient aristocracy may not, perhaps, be kept up with the same baronial splendour, or rude or profuse hospitality, as in days of yore. But manners are changed. The taste for a country life has declined. The luxurious owner may have other mansions that are preferable, or may relish the society, the pleasures, the refined dissipation of cities, more than his ancestors were

---

* This last also applies to the shipping-interest. But as to this question—involving, as I believe it does, matters beyond the mere profit or loss of the individuals engaged in it—my information is too limited to allow me to hazard an opinion. But after all the complaints on this head, it certainly may be observed that, by the Parliamentary returns for this year, more ships are built, and more tonnage registered, than at any previous period.

wont to do; or may have wasted his patrimony at the gaming-table. Such accidents do happen.

Where one hereditary house or family, however, falls into decay, half a dozen others shall be pointed out which were not known in the rank of affluence half a dozen years back. Every one migrates, at some particular part of the year, to foreign capitals, to watering-places, &c. A poor people are stationary. The country gentlemen exclaim "*they are ruined!*" that is, their tenants are not always able to pay the rent that is "in the bond,"—to fulfil engagements entered into under other circumstances. But ride to a covert-side in any county in the kingdom, during the hunting-season, and you will find some fifty or two hundred of these ruined gentlemen, mounted on horses with a dash of the Arabian blood in them, averaging in value from fifty to two hundred guineas. Each of these ruined gentlemen has got a stud, which he rides as if he might afford the loss of a horse now and then. Where else could this be afforded? No other body of ruined gentry in Europe could do it. Attend a popular race-course*—carriages will be found to have as-

* For horses of good pedigree and performance, from one to 4000 guineas is not an unusual price. This may be about four times what some French Dukes have wherewithal to live upon for the whole year.

sembled in countless thousands. There are large cities, that have grown up within a few years, whose style of buildings is minutely handsome, decorated to attract the eye, and which are designed solely for amusement, and are supported splendidly on the casual superfluities of those who are in search of pleasure or variety. Such cities are Brighton, Bath, Cheltenham, &c.

But a metropolis, especially one such as ours, which is not supported by a gorgeous court or a vast military establishment, will not be a bad index of the wealth of an empire. Where is there another London—this capital of an impoverished state ?—Is it not a kingdom rather than a city ?—For, perhaps, a hundred miles of its interminable streets, one may walk within almost a continued range, on either hand, of storehouses filled, for the most part, to the very doorways, with every imaginable variety of clothing, food, furniture, jewellery, plate, &c. Why, the contents of these shops would purchase the fee simple of the revenues of some very respectable states ! Many of the owners of these shops have their villas in the country, whither they retire after the business of the day is over, and where they live very often more like aristocrats than retail dealers.

" But there are no buyers," say those who

take another view of these matters. "The unfortunate shopman is closing his accounts, and must soon inevitably close his doors," &c. &c. But there are plenty of capitalists in the City, who are daily racking their brains to find out some new description of enterprize wherein to embark their money, and who would inevitably possess themselves of these unsaleable commodities, (if they really were unsaleable,) and would freight a fleet with them, and find a market for them somewhere else; for the greater part would be useful or in request in any region of the world.

Are the buildings, public or private, of this commercial centre and common mart of all nations, falling into decay, or lessening in number? On the contrary, great expense continues to be gone to, in throwing down whole streets, in order to erect in their place a better-adapted, more lofty, spacious, and a superior style of architecture. Hundreds of these more resemble palaces than private dwellings, and are only calculated for incomes of a very large amount. Nor are these gratifying signs of a prosperous condition, and of an abundant means, to be witnessed only in particular quarters: the interior, and the whole circumference, present a continuous and similar picture. It is new cities that are creating around the old one, while the latter is reconstructing after a more convenient and modern fashion. These are not the evidences of wealth—they are wealth itself.*

But those who maintain the converse, not unusually answer such statements as the above by saying—"*We are living on credit—we are spending our capital.*"

But this is impossible. It is one of the monstrous absurdities which sometimes pass current as argument. *A private individual cannot spend his principal, or even anticipate his income, without borrowing from some other individual, in money or goods* (which includes credit). Neither can a NATION, without *borrowing, in money or goods,* from SOME OTHER NATION. *Have we done so?* On the contrary, our merchants give long credits to foreign merchants; and OUR CAPITALISTS HAVE, SINCE THE WAR, LENT TO OTHER NATIONS, OR ADVANCED FOR FOREIGN SPECULATIONS,

* That wherewith any of these structures must be raised, consists of labour, bricks, iron, timber, &c. The brick-maker may overreach the timber-merchant, or the timber-merchant the brick-maker; or the stock-broker, for whom the mansion shall have been designed, may ruin himself, by a false calculation, before it become ready for his reception. Nevertheless, the property of which the mansion is composed, is no more unreal or fictitious than is the mansion itself when constructed.

BETWEEN ONE AND TWO HUNDRED MILLIONS STERLING.

There is another phenomenon peculiar to England. Let a dissolution of Parliament take place; and, presently, actually hundreds of our ruined gentry, or junior nobles, (who clamour occasionally for protecting duties,) will be ready to deposit, in their bankers' hands, as much as ten, fifty, or even a hundred thousand each, for the honour of representing a particular place or county. This is inconsistent with any other but a state of excessive opulence.

All these things prove, to demonstration, as it appears to me, that the aggregate wealth at present accumulated amongst us greatly transcends what it ever before was, and far surpasses any thing now or heretofore possessed by any other community of any other age or country.

That partial distresses, of a poignant nature, irregular repartition of the taxes, and serious embarrassment or confusion of the financial system exist, will be generally admitted. Some of these are attributable to the fluctuations from which commerce can never be exempt; some to sudden changes, of wide influence, (inevitable or otherwise,) but some of the effects of which will of themselves gradually subside; others, however, (and these, perhaps, the most important) being remedial, and demanding the correction of a powerful government. And having ample means available, and an administration which has already shewn, by signal triumphs in the cause of good sense and justice, what it can and will be disposed to do, I, for one, can see no earthly reason for despairing of the perfect health and invigorated power of the state. Neither, therefore, can I see any sufficient ground, because these corrections cannot be instantaneously applied, for foregoing, in the interim, any course of policy which the prospective interests of the empire may be deemed to require.

It is generally supposed that the country is now more burdened with debt than it ever was before, since the origin of national loans.* *I venture to maintain the entire fallacy of that position, on the following grounds :—*

Burdens of this nature, whether public or pri-

---

* The writers who treat of the progress of the national debt, usually dwell on the amount from time to time nominally contracted for, rather than upon the sum of interest or annuity payable on it. But the important fact is, the interest. For instance, a hundred years ago Government security gave about 6 or 6½ per cent. annuity. The nation then owed between fifty and sixty millions. But that sum was really equal to about 100,000,000 at the reduced interest of the present time of 3¾ per cent.

vate, can only be relatively estimated by comparison with the income of the debtor.

We will take four periods :—after the *Succession War*, 1716; conclusion of the American war, 1783; the commencement of the late wars, 1793; and the present time.

The *average revenue* of the first period (1716) may be put at £.4¾,000,000; the annuity to the public creditor, payable out of it, being nearly £.3½,000,000.

Average revenue of the second period (1783), £.12,000,000. Annuity to the public creditor, £.9,000,000.

Third period (1793). Revenue, £.17,000,000; annuity to the public creditor, £.10,000,000.

Average revenue of recent years, £.50,000,000. Annuity to the public creditor, £.28,000,000.

It appears, then, that the annuity (or *interest*) to be deducted, amounted, in the

First period to nearly three-fourths of the income.
Second „ to three-fourths of the income.
Third „ to two-thirds of the income.
Fourth „ to less than three-fifths of the income.

It is, therefore, manifest, that the interest

payable to the public creditor bore a materially heavier proportion to the revenue, in the three former periods, than in the fourth or present one.*

Then, with respect to the *surplus* revenue, the surplus of the present time is about twenty-fold greater than in the first-mentioned period—the population having only trebled.† (Average price of corn then about 40*s*.)

The surplus now is about sevenfold greater than in 1783, and three times greater than in 1793; (the population not being increased in the same proportion, nor even doubled—having been, in 1793, 15,000,000.)

---

* See also last note of the Appendix.

† The population of Russia is now said to be 58,000,000 in *Europe*. In the beginning of the eighteenth century it was stated at 12,000,000. This would make the increase, during one hundred years, 46,000,000; but this has been chiefly by conquest; while our's has advanced 16,000,000 without conquest. The following is from *Mr. Malthus* on the topic of population:—

"I am perfectly ready to acknowledge, with the writers of old, that it is not extent of territory but extent of population that measures the power of states. It is only as to the mode of obtaining a vigorous and efficient population that I differ from them.......The power of a country to increase its resources or defend its possessions must depend principally upon its efficient population, which is of an age to be employed effectually in agriculture, commerce, or war."

The greater the population, the greater the means of bearing or paying off incumbrances; unless when a population is labouring under a vicious system—under extraneous evils, as Ireland has been.

Finally, the population of the United Kingdom has *trebled* within about a century; the revenue has become *twelve* times more than it then was (1716); and the interest on the debt *nine* times greater, (28, 3½.) It is, therefore, impossible to deny that the incumbrances are now *proportionately* less than they *then* were. It is clear, also, from the same data, that the income of the state has been *gaining* upon the *incumbrances* during the past hundred years.*

If any one had asserted, in the reign of George the First, that in *another century* the ordinary annual revenue would equal in amount the *principal* of the debt, which was then considered to weigh so overwhelmingly† on the

* In reality, however, the gross income at present collected (including tithes, poor and church rates, &c.) amounts to £70,000,000; and, therefore, is probably about *fourteen* times greater than the gross sum collected in 1716: while the debt is advanced in the proportion of only *nine* to one. Poor-rates, in 1716, were half a million.

† It may not be unworthy of observation, that the periods during which this country seems to have made the

nation, he would have obtained no credit. Yet such has been the fact.

This is attributable to the increased industry and wealth of England and of Europe—to the consequent necessity of a larger quantity of circulating medium—to the increased produce of gold and silver mines, especially in America.

All those causes are operating more powerfully now, by many degrees, and through a far wider extent, than they were a hundred years ago. The persons who take alarm about the possible *increase* of the national debt, forget that it does not follow that the income is to be *stationary*.

If the debt should amount to £.1600,000,000 instead of £.800,000,000, and the income become £.100,000,000 instead of £.50,000,000, we should not be more deeply involved than we now are. The greater part of people, however, think that our incumbrances will infallibly increase, and our means diminish;—that the body politic is afflicted with an incurable atrophy;—that we are living luxuriously and extravagantly on a fictitious basis, the credit we derive from

---

most rapid strides in commercial greatness and political power, were those of war,—the seven years' war, and the last.

each other; that we are reciprocally consuming each other's means; and, in short, that a process is actually going on amongst us, not very dissimilar from that which we are told was mutually inflicted by the celebrated Kilkenny cats!

If the revenue of the country were to increase during the next hundred years, in the ratio that it has done during the last, it would amount, in 1930, to four or five hundred millions per annum. I do not say that it will; but I should like to know the reason why it may not.*

But to return from these speculations. So far from having any gloomy apprehensions, I am most sanguine on the subject of the national resources. As for the debt—even though no progress be made in paying it off, its pressure must become gradually lighter, in proportion to the increasing introduction of the precious metals; to the increasing industry and wealth of all the civilized nations; the consequent necessity of an increased circulating medium every where, and the *high prices* which must follow.

---

* It is not at all necessary that gold or silver to that amount should be introduced into circulation. We make use ourselves, EVEN NOW, of twenty-five millions of paper-money. In Russia, at present, there is scarcely anything else but paper-money to be seen.

As yet, there is probably a fourth part of the national property which does not pay to the exchequer its fair proportion of what is required for the purposes of the state.

There is a third part of the empire (Ireland), which now renders only a third part of what it will be enabled to pay before fifty years pass away. The twenty or thirty thousand men, which have been kept up in that country at great cost, for the maintenance of discord and poverty, will, ere long, be in a great part unnecessary.—The revenue of India advanced, during the government of the Marquess of Hastings, six millions sterling. "There is every just ground to reckon upon its progressive augmentation." . . . . . "*The clear Indian surplus to be henceforth exhibited, is estimated by me* (says Lord Hastings) *at four millions sterling yearly. It will probably be more ample.*" There is a commerce of inestimable promise about, probably, to be fully opened with 300,000,000 of Asiatics. America will recover from her revolutions, and eventually must afford a great field for commercial interchange. Some of our own colonies, the Cape, New Holland, will progressively rise to consequence, and become, for a long time, important markets to us. All these things taken into consideration, the prospect must be considered substantially good;—provided the progress of

European affairs shall not be interfered with, by the too great preponderancy of any one power. This would, of course, change the whole aspect and complexion of our calculations, and necessarily put to hazard the best-founded anticipation.

IV.

The *past* is always, of course, a safer and easier topic than the future. In reference to the former, *cause and effect,* as well as the opinions of others, are already developed, and more or less incontrovertible.

But the *future* is the *province of conjecture.* And those who meddle with it, must lay their account with being taunted as erroneous or visionary predictors, however correct the ideas thrown out may eventually prove.

When unforeseen delays occur, or when what has been suggested as a probable consequence does not forthwith come to pass, then those whose information or impressions are vague or carelessly taken up, at once set down the whole matter as a fallacy.

Such was last year the fate of the anticipations by so many indulged in (amongst others by the writer of these pages), relative to the perils which were supposed to await the Ottoman power.

In reality, however, if the integrity of the Moslem dominion in Europe shall, as a consequence of the pending conflict, be violated—

Whether such a consummation shall arrive, one, two, or more years, sooner or later, seems to be very much of a secondary moment, and but little calculated to diminish or increase the importance of the event in its international bearings. It is, I imagine, the vocation of statesmen to *carry forward their views*, and demand, with unswerving sternness, and at all hazards, security for the future? they cannot dare be content with the safety of the present moment, or with that species of prosperity which may depend upon the will of other governments.

That event (the overthrow of the Moslem dominion) seems on the eve of taking place; and, abstractedly, it is most desirable that so desolating and abhorrent a rule should perish. The great question still remains,—to whom shall the spoils, whether in point of territory, influence, or power, belong?

Whether a view should not rather be had to the eventual or gradual readmission of the Christian natives into their ancient proprietoryship? Whether the change shall merely be, that of dislodging from their military positions one horde of conquerors, to give place only to another; more humane it is true*, but scarcely less despotic, and, in the main, not a vast deal more civilised? Whether it shall be permitted to dash the lofty ruin suddenly from its base, instead of preparing the way for a more gradual process of demolition, through which the fragments may be removable, without endangering the stability of more costly neighbouring structures.

But to speak in a literal sense—the substance of what was advanced by the writer, when the topic was even more mooted than at present, may be comprised under four heads, viz.—1. THAT *the disruption of the triple alliance (for as such may essentially be regarded the separate hostility on the Danube) was to be traced to a policy of aggrandisement.*—2. THAT *negotiation, unaccompanied by some imposing display of force by the neutral powers, would probably fail of success.*—3. THAT *if the assailants should be allowed their own time for seizing on and establishing them-*

* "The fortune of a Russian Nobleman (says Malthus) is measured by the number of boors that he possesses, which *in general* are saleable, like cattle, and not *adscripti glebæ*. His revenue arises from a capitation on all the males." *Are these the people,* with their autocratic Government, their occult and unscrupulous policy, their military colonies, their universally military system, *to whom* the freedom and regeneration of Southern Europe can be safely entrusted?

selves in certain formidable vantage positions, it might become a more onerous task to dislodge than to have checked them in an earlier stage of the conflict.*—4. *Finally,* THAT *failing to resort promptly to a vigorous line of action might imminently compromise the eventual security of British interests, and the proximate balance of power as yet existing in Europe.*

Such was the main purport of the Essay "On the Designs of Russia."

The writer further attempted to trace some similitude † to the desperate concatenation of events which, in the case of *two contingent circumstances,* might be within the range of occurrence. These two circumstances were—*Ireland* being allowed to continue an arena for hostile factions and religious dissension, and *Russia* being allowed to continue for a few years an unmolested career of aggrandisement.

The Catholic Relief Bill may be considered, I would venture to hope, as the earnest of an assured remedy for the first of these unfortu-

---

* "To drive the Muscovite eagles back over the Danube or Pruth may not be so easy a task as to have checked their flight ere they had passed those barriers."—*Evans,* p. 70, (1828).

† Expressly "*hypothetical.*"—See also note in the Appendix, page 142.

nate contingencies; and the same wisdom which extricated the country in the one instance, may, no doubt, be yet more implicitly relied on with respect to the other.

V.

"*As the income of most of the Russian nobility is derived from the sale of the produce of their estates for exportation* (total six millions' worth), *and as a war with England produces a total stagnation of exports, it will easily be seen how unpopular and disadvantageous a rupture with this country must ever prove.*"*. . . . . "*Where we annually take from her so large a portion of her produce, she surely ought, in fairness and reciprocity, to take from us a certain return, unfettered by vexatious duties and restrictions.*"

Our relative interest in the maintenance of this commerce is of a very different nature. We take from them three and a half millions' worth of their raw produce, while they take from us two millions in manufactures. In case of a war one half, perhaps, of the above-named portion of our manufactures

* Captain Jones, (R. N.) p. 546.

would continue to be smuggled into Russia. The naval stores, tallow, &c. thrown back upon the hands of the Russian magnates, we could procure equally well, and with little or no inconvenience, from Sweden, Norway, America, &c. The only material inconvenience would be of a personal nature—that which would arise to the particular class of merchants trading to Riga and St. Petersburgh*; to whom, of course, every fair

---

* These merchants have sent forth a pamphlet deprecatory, of course, of any collision with Russia, entitled, "A FEW WORDS ON OUR RELATIONS WITH RUSSIA; *including Remarks on a recent publication by Colonel de Lacy Evans.*" The first chapter of this production runs thus:—"*Reasons for writing—Semi-hostile disposition of the Ministry towards the Russians.*" "For some time past, a considerable number of persons, some politicians who tremble for the fall of the old idol in politics—'the balance of power,' or resent the insult to the nation supposed to be implied in the blockade of the Dardanelles; some merchants who trade with the Turks; and some editors of journals who trade in incense to current prejudices, have been working to push this country into a quarrel with Russia." This passage, which is evidently addressed to the most uninformed, can require no comment. The writer or writers are extremely angry with his Majesty's Government for thwarting the designs (or intending to do so), of his Imperial Majesty the Czar!—The greater the extent of the Russian dominion, the weaker it must be, &c. &c., with a series of other equally notable paradoxes.—This pamphlet is entirely Russian in its spirit; and, in point of fact, independent of the manifest motive

degree of consideration is due, consistent with paramount national interests.

From the same highly-informed naval officer (Captain Jones) I insert the following, which is the more entitled to deep attention, as being the result of personal and professional observation:

"Russia would also have a most excellent nursery for seamen, as every necessary article for building and rigging ships would soon spontaneously flow to the banks of the before-enumerated rivers, as well as to their common port, the Liman.

"In point of fact, has not the practicability of this, on the largest scale, been already proved by the creation on the Black Sea of a military marine, comprising ships of one hundred and ten guns, which, when brought to their lightest draught of water, will swim deeper than the heaviest laden merchantmen. These ships of war, although brought down on camels from Cherson, Nicholief, &c., as low as Kilbourin, have at the latter place been always fitted for sea; so that it is absurd to talk, as is now commonly done, of these shoals forming an insuperable objection to the Liman being appli-

---

it is understood to be from the pen of some clever persons at the head of the Baltic trade, who are, by birth and connexion, more Muskovite than English.

cable to the purposes of commerce; for, on the contrary, the Liman presents tenfold the advantages to Russia, which the lagunes of Venice ever did to that commercial and haughty republic. In short, without going into detail, were the commercial properties of the Liman and its rivers properly understood, I cannot see where the mercantile prosperity and enterprise of Russia need stop. Not only might she enjoy a most profitable trade on the Black Sea, on that of Azof, and the Mediterranean, but extend her commerce to every part of the globe. Instead of the sands at the mouth of the Dnieper, and the reported dangerous navigation of the Black Sea, proving obstacles, they would form the best possible school for making hardy and experienced seamen, similar to our north-country sailors, who are acknowledged to be the best in the world, because most of their ports are rendered difficult to approach on account of bars and shoals; and the whole navigation to London is one of the most dangerous and difficult in existence, and, consequently, calls forth all the energy and enterprise of which man is capable.

"*So that, in time, a numerous and hardy race of native seamen would be formed merely by the trade on the Black Sea and that of Azof.* These two seas present an amazing extent of coast, when it is considered that the former is six hundred miles in length and three hundred and thirty broad in the widest part, and one hundred and forty-two in the narrowest; while the latter is one hundred and eighty-six miles in length, and ninety in breadth. *Both possess that which renders them invaluable as a nursery for good seamen, namely, every description of coast, depth of water, and variety of currents.* It has been well observed, by an intelligent author, that the country which possesses the greatest line of coast must ever prove superior in point of seamen. Now, including the seven hundred and eighty-six miles, the length of the Black Sea, and that of Azof, it must be remembered that the extent of coast, without regarding sinuosities, is at least one thousand six hundred miles, nearly all the trade of which would soon fall into the hands of Russia; for the Turks, from indolence and natural aversion to the sea, would soon abandon it to them. *No other nation, supposing all restrictions were abolished, would ever be able to compete with them, on account of the easy rate at which the Russians could build, fit, and sail their vessels; the empire producing within itself every necessary article for both building and equipment at an extraordinarily low price, and in the greatest abundance,* while the natives are accustomed to live on the hardest fare. But should they become refined, still all ordinary provisions are extremely reasonable; and *there is little doubt that Russian ships could be built and navigated at nearly half the expense of those of any other nation*, particularly in the Black Sea.

"Indeed, when I survey the maritime resources of this great empire, I cannot persuade myself that Russia is not destined to become a great naval and commercial power. However, from the existing prejudices on the part of the natives to any thing connected with the sea, there cannot be a doubt that much time will elapse, before such a material change can be produced in their habits as to verify my prediction. *But should the present or a future sovereign be duly impressed with the importance of the subject, it is impossible to say how soon such an alteration might be effected, particularly when we consider the acknowledged docility of temper which all the common natives possess.*"—p. 384.*

If such be the maritime capabilities with reference only to the situation of Russia before the present war, what may not be anticipated, if she obtain a port, or even only an ascendant influence in the Marmora?

Between the maintenance of a proximate ba-

* See also Leckie, Pasley, Stewart (State of the Nation), Gibbon, Polybius, and, in short, every work which touches on the subject.

lance of strength between the confederate civilized nations, and the establishment of an ascendant empire, and eventually of *one dominion,* there is no probable medium. An ascendant continental state will always be disposed to direct against us, and against our commerce and marine, the chief weight of its hostility and force, because it is from us that the last resistance to supremacy is to be looked for. The American revolutionary war, which raised the national debt to above 250,000,000*l.*, was not for the maintenance of the balance of power; neither was this the motive of the French revolutionary war, which added still further to the debt 200,000,000*l.* This seems to have had for its object the repression of democratical opinion or popular institutions. The war entered into in 1803 was, it is true, for the balance of power, and even for political existence,—national independence being then verging, in the greater part of Europe, to the last stage of peril. But this great struggle was a direct consequence of the impolitic, or, at all events, unskilfully conducted war of 1793. An imprudent, or unnecessary war, may sometimes be redeemed by the vigour and ability with which it is waged. Such was not the case with respect to the contest last named; but such might be the case in the present instance, because never, at any former era, were such capable war ministers at the head of the public affairs. For a period of at least two-thirds of the late twenty years' wars, our able parliamentary leaders evinced more constancy than talent in the disposal of the military resources of the country : a fruitless exhaustion of treasure was, to an incredible extent, the consequence. If a war with Russia should be a result of the present state of things, we may be well persuaded that one pound will go further in its prosecution than three heretofore. It is also satisfactory to know, that not a man need be added to our colonial garrisons (the Ionian, perhaps, excepted) ;—that instead of 140,000* sailors and marines, 50,000 for that arm would suffice (namely, 30,000 added to the present strength) ; and that no 100,000 militia, or 200,000 volunteers or fencibles, to line our shores with, could be requisite. The four points of collision would probably be—the eastern shore of the Baltic, during a short season of the year ; the eastern shore of the Mediterranean ; Persia ; the north-western frontier of India. The charges and expenditure for the two latter would fairly have to be defrayed by our eastern possessions.

The merchants whose transactions are with

---

* 1813.

St. Petersburgh and Riga, and those who have lent to Russia ten or twelve millions of money, will probably do their best, through the press, to lull opinion on this question, be the conduct of the Russian Cabinet what it may. Others, who believe that in arithmetic, political economy, and the calculations of immediate pecuniary gain or loss, are comprised, not a *part*, but the *whole* science of government, will coincide with those who are actuated by direct personal considerations. Numbers of the useful school of economists seem influenced by the amiable delusion, that henceforth the passions and ambition will be alien to the resolves of cabinets, and to human conduct.

In the mean time, it is sanguinely rumoured that General Diebitsch has halted his columns, consented to an armistice, and that peace is about to be concluded.

It is, no doubt, probable that *hostilities* may for the present cease, or may *have* ceased, because to carry on hostilities two parties are necessary, and one of the present belligerents is scarcely any longer in a condition to continue the conflict.

A treaty of peace, imposing moderate conditions, with all the formalities of diplomacy and of neutral guarantee, would no doubt be desirable; but the final withdrawal of armies and evacuation of fortresses would be better. When Adrianople, Sizeboli, Bourgas, Varna, Silistria, Brailow, Trebisond, and Kars, are no longer garrisoned by the Czar—when the victorious banners now waving over the shores of the Egæan and Marmora, and on the towers of Erzeroum, shall have been carried back beyond the Pruth and the Araxes—then there may be an interval and a prospect of security and repose for Europe.

"But granting* that the autocrat merely insists on the independence of the principalities,—this is precisely what was done with respect to the Crimea. What was the result? Briefly, afterwards, the khaun was compelled, by one means or another, humbly to lay his ostensible sovereignty at the feet of the Russian Empress. Such was also the preliminary to occupation of the Kuban and several other countries, now forming part of New Russia, as appears by the Article III. of the treaty of Kainarga, 1774. '*All the Tartar people,* (says that treaty,) *those of Crimea, Budgiac, of the Kuban, the Edissans, Geambouiluks and Edisschkuls, shall, without any exception, be acknowledged by the two Empires as* FREE NATIONS, *and entirely independent of any foreign power, and shall be governed by their own*

---

* *Designs of Russia,* p. 44.

sovereign of the race of Gingis-Khan, elected and raised to the throne by all the Tartar people; who shall govern them according to their ancient laws and usages, rendering no account whatever to any foreign power,' &c. &c. These solemn guarantees were soon after found to be no better than waste paper."

ON THE

PRACTICABILITY OF AN INVASION

OF

BRITISH INDIA.

THE character of the last year's campaign on the Danube dissipated, in a great degree, the apprehensions at first created in some parts of Europe by the war. The invaders certainly gained no military glory; but they remained, nevertheless, at the close of the operations, in possession of an acquired territory, about equal in extent to the British empire. These acquisitions lay in Armenia, Wallachia, Moldavia, and Bulgaria *. The three former are uudergoing an

* It was generally supposed that the Russians had been entirely driven out of Bulgaria. The fact, however, was, that they retained in that province a tract of one hundred and forty miles long, by (on an average) about thirty-five broad: covered by the entrenched line of Paravadi and

organization, very much, to appearance, that of Russian provinces; and are now actually furnishing auxiliary contingents of troops to the Czar's army.

Ample time for mediation has ineffectually passed away, since the commencement of the contest; instead of restricting itself, the sphere of action has been extended; the commerce of the maritime neutrals has become subject to increased vexations; a flagrant infraction of the law of nations * has been persevered in; the forces of the Sultan have just sustained signal defeats, both in Europe and Asia, and those of his enemy are closing upon him with a corresponding progress.

Bazardjick. The Principalities exceed England in area. The requisition of troops stated as the quota of Wallachia is 10,000. The conduct of some of those native levies is commended in one of the late despatches of Count Diebitsch; and by General Geismar.

* The blockade of the Dardanelles is not a blockade of Constantinople, but of entire seas—of countless miles of coast in Europe and Asia.

The above and the preceding page were in manuscript before the passage of the Balkan was effected—it did not appear essential to make any alteration.

These successes (important as they are) were, however, slower of achievement than was originally anticipated; but, the *war is not over;* the issue of one campaign, or the incompetency of a superseded general-in-chief, hardly afforded a sufficient ground for estimating the real strength or resources of the contending states. It was, therefore, too soon, and is still too soon, for those who hazarded predictions on either side of the question, to triumph in the fulfilment of their opinions.

But amongst the topics connected with the pending war, or with the progress of the Russian arms or influence in the East, there are none to us of a more direct consequence, than those respecting any serious hostility from that source to the British dominion, ascendancy, or commerce in the East.

The celebrated French political economist, *M. Baptiste Say*, has written an Essay a very few years ago, the professed object of which is, to "*dispel illusions*," which he conceives exist on the continent, relative to the supposed facility of expelling the English from India, and which *Baptiste Say.*

he apprehends are "*likely to involve Europe in a vain expenditure of blood and treasure.*"—Even the "*governments of the continent,*" he says, share in this erroneous opinion, and imagine, "*that they have only to appear in arms* (in India), and *overthrow* (there the) *hated and unstable power* (of Britain). *This was Buonaparte's intention by the expedition to Egypt, and it* HAS TWENTY TIMES OCCUPIED THE CABINET OF ST. PETERSBURG."

"European forces," he says, "could only be sent by land; and let any one calculate the delay, the expense, and the loss which must attend an army in such an expedition! Not to speak of the nations it would have to fight with on its road, of the men, horses, and artillery lost in the burning sands, the trackless swamps, and impassable rivers," &c.

Herein is comprised the sum of the local or topographical information on which the Professor founds his dictum on this great operation. To the history of "Mr. James Mill" he declares himself indebted for the chief part of his statements. Mere professional soldiers, whatever degree of practical experience they may be possessed of, usually require more detailed and authenticated data, and trust less to their genius.

1. What particular line of country Mr. Say refers to, he does not state. But as that which it is intended to trace in the sequel of these pages, passes through the territories of three states, (Khiva*, Bokhara, Caubul,) the climates of which are spoken of in terms of admiration, as "*delightful, salubrious, and invigorating,*" by the Russian and English envoys and officers who have lately visited them, it may be conjectured, that the sands do not burn so very intensely as to destroy an invading army.

2. Not a word about *trackless swamps* is to be found in the lately published volumes descriptive of this line of country†. Nor are swamps of any extent usually to be met with on dry and elevated table-lands.

3. It so happens, also, that there is *no* considerable river crossing the line just mentioned.

---

* Elphinstone, Mouravief, Meyendorf, &c.

† Since writing the above, I met with this one line in Meyendorf, p. 105, " On ne connait pas de marécages dans la Steppe."

The only body of water to be classed as such, in that whole tract, being the Oxus; along the banks of which, or embarked upon which, it has been suggested, as will be shown, that troops might proceed without any prospect of material loss. Rivers, however, of magnitude they would eventually have to meet, on the western boundary of our dependency—the Indus and Punjaub. But if Mr. Say had thought it proper (as a qualification for pointing out the military errors of Napoleon) to have turned over a few leaves (for instance) of Frederick, or of any military writer whatever,—he would have discovered that rivers are deemed the *least** impassable of all barriers; that those who have trusted to them for defence have in-

* "To defend a river, on a long line, is generally hopeless." . . . . "The defence of rivers has always proved fruitless," says the eloquent and amply-instructed military historian—*Napier*.

Did the great rivers of Russia stop Napoleon's march to Moscow? Did the half dozen rivers of Spain—the Douro, Ebro, Esla, Pisuerga, &c.—arrest the rapid progress of Wellington, when he rushed, as it may be said, with his whole army, from the interior of Portugal to the summits of the Pyrenees?—And yet those rivers had for their defence above a hundred thousand French soldiers, with fortified posts upon them, capable of sustaining a siege.

variably been deceived; and that rivers never yet stopped an enterprise of consequence, or a commander of the most moderate talent.

Buonaparte may be considered to have twice *Napoleon.* projected an invasion of India—in 1798—1808: the first from Egypt, the latter through Constantinople; or to descend, in junction with a Russian force, down one of the rivers of that empire into the Euxine or Caspian. The attempt from Egypt could scarcely, under any circumstances, have succeeded, so long as the communication with France, and the means of obtaining reinforcements from thence, were cut off by the English fleet. Napoleon counted, it would seem, on a preconcerted and nearly simultaneous expedition to Ireland, as calculated to free the Mediterranean from a portion of the British naval force.

Of the other, of which the French Officers sent into Persia were to be the precursors, had he not been attracted to Spain, and the alliance with Russia had continued, it is not so easy to calculate the result.

Of the earlier and far more problematical design, twenty years afterwards he deliberately writes thus in his Memoirs:—

"The principal object of the French expedition to the East was to check the power of the English. The army which was to change the destiny of India was to march from the Nile. The revolution of India was likely to be more or less near, according as the chances of war should prove more or less fortunate, and the inhabitants of Arabia and Egypt should be more or less favourably disposed," &c.

He goes on to state the views he entertained, and the occurrences which rendered success more difficult; and concludes by observing, that

"The provinces of the Ottoman empire, in which Arabic is spoken, heartily prayed for a change, and waited for a leader. We might, if fortunate, have been on the Euphrates by the middle of the summer, with 100,000 auxiliaries, who would have had a reserve of 25,000 French veterans, some of the best troops in the world, with a numerous train of artillery. Constantinople would then have been menaced; and if an amicable connexion could have been formed with the Porte, we might have crossed the Desert, and marched upon the Indus by the end of autumn."

One may be disposed to doubt the soundness of these views; we shall, however, hesitate to do so, on calling to mind the long-practised and profound genius which conceived and acted upon them.

I have not met with any explanation in the "Memoirs of Napoleon," relative to the precise intention of General Gardanne's mission to Persia; or to the plan subsequently mooted at Tilsit. The conduct of Gardanne and his numerous suite leaves not a doubt that the object was to carry the war into Asia. The particulars, however, are involved in uncertainty. The following, in reference to it, I take from the 'Quarterly Review' of 1813:—

"The treaty of Tilsit, and the subsequent armistice between Russia and the Ottoman Porte, placed Persia at the mercy of the three Allied Powers. Nothing ever transpired as to the secret stipulations regarding Persia; but it was generally understood on the Continent, that Oudinot had been actually selected to proceed with a corps of 12,000 men, with all the baggage and equipments necessary for such an expedition. Two routes from Tilsit were sufficiently commodious for such an enterprise—first, by *descending* the *Volga to Astracan*, embarking at that port, and crossing the Caspian to some of the ports of Mazenderaun, near to the Persian capital. This province, with its impervious forests, rugged mountains, deep ravines, and narrow passes, is so strong as to be capable of being held by a small European corps against the united armies of all Persia. The second route was by descending the Dnieper into the Black Sea, thence proceeding up the Kuban to Circassia, and joining the Russian head-quarters at Teflis, in Georgia. Whether the object of this small corps was to unite with Russia, in order to subdue the northern provinces of Persia, or merely to ascertain the practicability of establishing positions, collecting magazines, and opening routes for a larger army, which was to follow, or whatever the design might have been, it was necessarily abandoned on account of the Spanish revolution of 1808, and the Austrian campaign of 1809."

But we are not without more specific reports as a basis—the statements of those who have been selected by their respective governments for high office, political, military, or diplomatic, connected with the countries referred to, or in missions to them. These, it will readily be conceded, claim altogether a superior attention, not only on account of their probable fitness and peculiar facilities for the acquisition of information, but because of the accordance also to be assumed as usually existing between the recorded opinions of persons so trusted and the policy of the cabinets whom they represent.

Likewise it is fairly to be assumed, that an indispensable regard to professional or public character, on the part of functionaries of this class, must afford strong personal motives and a guarantee for due consideration and correctness.

It is on these grounds, and as comprising the true foundation from which inferences may without temerity be drawn, that the following authorities have been consulted and quoted from.

Instructions, it appears, were given to various political agents, despatched by the Bengal Government, in 1809, into Central or Western Asia, pointing out to them, in general terms, the advantages to be anticipated from making every possible exertion to ascertain the nature and resources of those countries through which an invading European army might advance towards Hindoostan; and likewise sanctioning the employment, in the capacity of political assistants or surveyors, of any number of officers that might be deemed requisite to give full effect to this suggestion *. A great body of infor-

* Pottinger—Surveyor with the missions to Sinde and Persia, and resident at the Court of the Peishwa.

mation has been the fruit of these judicious precautions.

General Malcolm, having been thus instructed, and having been twice Plenipotentiary in Persia, must have had sources of intelligence of the most ample description. He states in his Political History, that "THE FRONTIER of the INDUS IS THE MOST VULNERABLE part of our EASTERN EMPIRE."—Again, "The designs (he says) of the French at this period were known to be directed with more than usual activity to that object (India); and the means which they possessed for their accomplishment, though irregular and difficult of combination, were far from contemptible."

From the policy of Lords Wellesley and Minto it appears, that not a doubt existed in their minds as to the designs of France upon India. That, however, is abundantly confirmed by Napoleon himself. Neither of these Governor-Generals appears to have been in the least aware of there being any insurmountable obstacles of a local nature to the approach of a hostile army, even though the march must have lain through Persia.—To the same effect more than one passage may be met with in the Marquess Wellesley's History of the Mahratta War.

Colonel Macdonald Kinneir was one of those employed by Sir John Malcolm in the inquiries pointed out, relative to the nature of the countries included between Europe and India, and the obstacles or facilities for an enterprise against us in that quarter. This able officer subsequently became, and is now, our representative at the court of Teheraun. His authority on this topic must be of the greatest weight.

"Although the possession (he says) of that country (Hindostan) can be but of trifling advantage to an European power which does not command a maritime communication, it might be the object of Russia to deprive us of what it considers to be one of the chief sources of our strength.

"It is, perhaps, unnecessary (he continues) to remark that this dissertation was written before the downfal of Napoleon and the eventful changes in Europe, which, BY THE AGGRANDIZEMENT OF RUSSIA, HAVE ENDANGERED THE SAFETY OF OUR EASTERN POSSESSIONS."

"It cannot, however (the same writer states), be denied that the Persians would seize with avidity any proposal of this nature—(an invasion of British India): the love of plunder, the example of Nadir Shah, and the idea which they have formed of the wealth and weakness of our Eastern possessions, would alike stimulate them to the undertaking.

"It was my determination, on quitting England, to visit all the countries through which *an European army might attempt the invasion of India*, and, in prosecution of this plan, to explore the north-eastern parts of Persia, and *the vast plains which stretch beyond the Oxus towards the confines of the Russian empire. . . . It were, doubtless, to be wished that we possessed some personal knowledge of the state and resources of so large and populous a kingdom* as Bokhara, which, from its situation, must ever be considered as A MOST IMPORTANT BARRIER TO THE ENCROACHMENTS OF RUSSIA TOWARDS OUR ORIENTAL POSSESSIONS."—*Memoir on Asia Minor.*

Colonel Kinneir admits that the idea of invading Hindostan by the Red Sea or Persian Gulf cannot be regarded as very feasible,—far otherwise, however, with respect to another line.

"In the year 1791 (he states), when it was expected that a rupture would take place between England and Russia, a plan for the invasion of India was presented by the Prince de Nassau to the Empress Catherine II. This project is said to have been drawn up by the celebrated M. D. St. Genie, who proposes, I understand (for I have not seen the plan), that the army should either march down the plain of the *Volga**, and CROSS THE CASPIAN SEA, or move through *Bokhara and Balk* to the Indus. *Of the many plans suggested for the invasion of Hindostan,* that of CROSSING THE CASPIAN, AND SAILING UP THE OXUS, APPEARS TO ME TO BE THE MOST EASY OF EXECUTION."

"The Oxus is navigable till within three or four days journey of Balk; but, previous to the embarkation of the army, boats must be con-

---

* Embarked upon the Volga—more eligibly,—since this magnificent river is navigable from near Moscow, through the most fertile regions of the empire, the whole way to Astrakan, on the Caspian. Steam-boats and vessels of a large burthen (two and three hundred tons) are employed upon it. The professors of the Greek persuasion are scrupulous in keeping the Lent. The quantity of fish consumed by the Russians is, therefore, very great. It is almost wholly supplied from the Caspian; and, by means of the Volga, is carried into the heart of the empire, and thence distributed to the more populous districts. For this branch of commerce alone a vast number of large vessels are required on the river,—in the estuary of which (below Astracan), and in the Caspian, the prolific sturgeon fisheries are carried on on so stupendous a scale. The sturgeon usually runs from *one thousand to twenty-three hundred pounds weight;* one of them frequently contains as much as one hundred and fifty pounds of roe, which constitutes the famed dish called *caviar.*

structured, and depôts of provisions must be formed. - - - This, indeed, is the only manner in which, in my opinion, India can ever be invaded with a prospect of success."

As to the necessity of constructing boats on the Oxus, that (*as will be seen by the reports of the Russian officers*) may not be necessary, at least to any extent. The natives, it appears, employ large boats upon it, and in considerable numbers, capable of carrying as many as six laden camels, and some even so many as fifty horses. In moving up the river towards Bokhara and Balk with merchandize, they track, with horses, in the same manner used in the internal navigation of this country.

Corroborative of the foregoing is the following, from "The SURVEY of ETON,"—originally Consul in Turkey, afterwards for several years Secretary to the British Embassy at Petersburg; subsequently in the employ of the *Russian Premier and Generalissimo*, POTEMKIN:—

"What might have been the event of such a war (1791) it is difficult to foresee; much conjecture may be made. I will only mention one circumstance, the naming of which is alarming, however it may be treated as romantic:—THE EMPRESS HAD FIRMLY RESOLVED TO ATTEMPT TO SEND AN ARMY THROUGH BOKHARA to Cashmere, to place the Mogul on the throne of India, and drive the British out of their possessions; and there were then in Russia, Frenchmen, who had been sent into these parts by M. de Vergennes, and who offered to conduct the army.

"When the British fleet was about to sail for the Baltic, to force the Empress to make peace, Prince Nassau, who was then in favour with her Imperial Majesty, presented a plan for sending an army through Bokhara to Cashmere, and thence to Bengal, to drive the English out of India."

"Little difficulty was foreseen in passing through *Bokhara;* it was even hoped, seeing the object was to re-establish on the throne of India a Prince of their religion, that they would be friendly to the enterprise: however, were they not, little apprehension was entertained of a people so disunited among themselves, and who tremble at the name of Russia.

"St. Genie pretended that there were passes through the mountains, and that he had people who had been in the country, sent by M. de Vergennes. He presented with his project a map, and a *march-route* for the army.

"They counted on being joined in the north of India by the discontented from all parts."

It will have been seen that the French also calculated on some yet remaining principle of allegiance supposed to exist towards the Imperial Family of Delhi.

Opinion of the Marquess of Hastings. "As to attack from abroad (says the Marquess of Hastings), the intention must be long previously discovered, so that India could not be found unprepared. The project would be futile, did it not embrace the calculation of disposition and ability in the inhabitants of India to facilitate the undertaking. Such an expectation would, in the existing position of affairs, be groundless. . . . . . There is not in the vicinity of that river's left bank (the Indus) any tribe from which an invader could look to encouragement*; on the contrary, the attempt of any secondary column to pass that river where its stream is united, and thereby to distract attention from the main body, which would hold a more northerly course, could not fail to experience serious and persevering obstruction from an energetic people."

---

* The Russian government by no means coincides with this opinion, if at least an inference may be drawn from the diplomatic intercourse now carrying on with the chiefs on the Indus.

This distinguished general officer was ten years commander-in-chief and governor-general of India; and yet he seems to have been quite unconscious of the complete security arising from "trackless swamps and impassable rivers," such as those which the learned French economist informs the world must bar the Indian frontier against an European army. The existence of any such insurmountable barrier appears to have escaped the contemplation of the Marquess:—his lordship's reliance having been placed rather on the supposition of a feeling of reciprocal interest, actuating the native princes, or on their insignificant means, if hostilely disposed,—and on the contentment of the people generally.

Lord Hastings, however, admits, that there is in India a principle, capable of superseding the most thorough conviction of interest. And of this class, he says, is a still remaining sense of loyalty, (" though antiquated,") which is felt to be due to the " House of Timour."

" It must be obvious (he adds), that should any *European potentate* aim at the subversion of the British establishment in India, it would not be with so absurdly extravagant a hope as the succeeding to a similar domination. To reduce Britain's strength, by depriving her of such sinews as India affords, would be the purpose. . . . . . : *While such a war-cry* (the restoration of the House of Timour) *would have been a call on the fealty of the sovereign of Oude, as professedly vizier of the empire, the claim upon him would have had the additional force of an ostensibly Mahommedan cause. The country contains at least six millions of inhabitants, every adult male of whom is provided with arms, and habituated to the use of them.* THE FORCE, HOWEVER IRREGULAR, CAPABLE TO BE THENCE COLLECTED IN THE REAR OF THE ARMY WITH WHICH WE WERE MEETING THE INVADER ON THE FRONTIER, WAS A SUBJECT NOT TO BE REVOLVED WITHOUT ANXIETY. *The knowledge of an insurrection behind them, to an extent which could not be ascertained, as our communication with the Lower Provinces would be precarious and interrupted, if not wholly cut off, would unavoidably agitate the minds, and diminish the confidence of the advanced troops.* I HAD OFTEN RUMINATED ON THAT CHANCE."

The late Governor-General then goes on to describe a sort of harmless Machiavellian scheme which he fell upon, in order to embroil the Vizier of Oude with the Moghul Emperor, by conferring on or inducing the former to assume the title of *King*, and so preventing the contingency of their coalescing against us, in the event of " attack from abroad :" for, as was anticipated, this assumption of royalty gave mortal offence to all the members of the (in fact) captive, but still proud and partially respected *Tartarian* dynasty.

Oude, however, is but a fraction of the multitude which people the subjugated peninsula. The Mahrattas alone had embodied (or were in the act of embodying) against us, even at so recent a period as that of his Lordship's government, as many as two hundred and thirteen thousand men, with an artillery of five hundred pieces.

In short, as to counting on security from foreign attack, as being likely, as yet at least, to arise, in any main degree, from the fealty or especial attachment of a population, so large a proportion of which still consists of armies vanquished and disbanded *by us,*—of freebooters whom we have *chastised and put down*—of military chiefs, of whom *we* have caused the personal ruin,—of the adherents of families from whom we may have but just wrested power, rank, even personal liberty: this undoubtedly seems, if one may be permitted to say it, a problematical ground for reliance, or for expectation of support. At all events, authorities are not agreed upon it. Besides, even if they were perfectly well disposed towards us, the total paucity of means, on the part of the states lying along the Indus, to offer serious obstruction to the ingress of a European force, can scarcely be a matter of doubt. The incohesive and fragile nature of the territorial or political power of *Runjeet Singh** (comprising Cashmere, Lahore, and Moultan) is very well known. And of the adjoining Rajpootana countries†, *Colonel Tod*, more than twenty years political resident in them, observes (in his magnificent work just published),—

Colonel Tod. "Can we suppose such denationalized allies are to be depended upon in emergencies? or, if allowed to retain a spark of their ancient moral inheritance, that it will not be kindled into flame against us when opportunity offers, instead of

* Present population of the dominions of the Lahore chief, 3,000,000.

† Population, 15,000,000.

lighting up the feeling of gratitude which yet exists towards us in these warlike communities?"

"*Must we* NOT *rationally look for re-action in some grand impulse*, which, by furnishing a signal instance of the mutability of power, may afford a lesson for the benefit of posterity?"

The eight Rajpoot states cover a vast space, immediately east of the valley of the Indus.

"This confederation of *feudatory states* extends (says Lord Hastings) in an unbroken chain quite to the Indus." And from these his Lordship anticipates, in case of need, a vigorous resistance to an invasion from the west. *Marquess of Hastings.*

Here, however, there is a conflicting evidence; Colonel Tod is at issue with his chief. *Colonel Tod.*

"The closest attention (he says) to their history proves, beyond contradiction, that they were *never capable of uniting even for their own preservation!* a breath, a scurrilous stanza of a bard, has severed their closest confederacies. No national head exists among them as amongst the Mahrattas; and each chief being master of his own house and followers, they are individually too weak to cause us any alarm."

"No FEUDAL government can be dangerous as a

neighbour: for defence, it has in all countries been found defective; and for aggression, totally inefficient. Let there exist between us the most perfect understanding and identity of interests; the foundation-step to which is to lessen the *galling*, and to us contemptible tribute, now exacted; enfranchise them from our *espionage* and *agency;* and either unlock them altogether from our dangerous embrace, or let the ties between us be such only as would ensure grand results—such as general commercial freedom and protection, with treaties of friendly alliance. Then, if a TATAR, or a RUSSIAN INVASION threatened our Eastern empire, fifty thousand Rajpoots would be no despicable allies."

"Let us, then, apply history to its proper use. We need not to turn to ancient Rome for illustration of the dangers inseparable from wide dominion and extensive alliances."—p. 196.

Frazer. The travels of Mr. Frazer* in Central Asia have perhaps thrown more light than those of any other person on the state of these hitherto comparatively unexplored regions. His last publication (1825), the valuable account of Khorasaun, contains the following statement:—

"In the geographical notices regarding *Khawresm*†

---

* This highly-informed public servant was then political assistant with the embassy to Caubul.

† The territory around Khiva, anciently, in fact, a chief central portion of Ghengis Khaun's dominion.

and Maweraulnehr (which are to be found in the Appendix), I have observed that the distance between the bay of Mangushluc, on the Caspian Sea, and Khiva, the present capital of Khawresm, is only ten days' journey of a caravan; and, in another part of the same, it will be found that the river *Amoo*, or Oxus (only one day's journey, with water-carriage, from the town of Khiva), is *navigable for boats the whole way from Balkh to Ourgunge* (a city about a day's journey from Khiva); and, as it flows through a level country, the channel is not likely to be much interrupted by rapids, or dangers of any kind. *From Balkh, and from Khoondooz (a town about two days' march from the river, higher up than Balk), there is a road to Caubul, which, I have reason to believe, is by no means very difficult.* It must, indeed, lead through the Hindoocooch, by Boot Baumian, and, consequently, over some lofty hills; but I could not procure any routes sufficiently distinct to give a good idea of its nature. As, however, this route to Caubul and India was constantly used in former times, *and is so even now*, it probably offers no serious obstacles; and the whole distance does not, I believe, exceed TWO HUNDRED AND FIFTY MILES*."—p. 238.

"From the tenor (Mr. Frazer says) of his work (that of the Russian Envoy to Khiva, 1820) the objects of the Russian Government are clear enough: they

---

* According to *Meyendorf*—twelve days' journey of a caravan, his informant being a merchant, who had travelled the road thirty times.

have endeavoured to conciliate the Toorkomaun tribes to the north of Astrabad; so that the commercial relations they encourage with them may not be disturbed, nor the tribes themselves take alarm when they establish posts upon the coast; and they have made the same attempt with the ruler of Khiva, gaining at the same time a certain degree of information respecting the local and political situation of that state, to enable them, should conciliatory means fail, to take the earliest opportunity of obtaining possession by force, first, of a footing on the coast, and then of Khiva itself. The author, in his work (M. Mouravief), not only points out the importance to Russia of such an entrepot, through which much of the commerce of the East would (he thinks) flow into that empire, but he discovers the weak points of the country, and the ease with which the conquest might be made; and, certainly, there is little doubt that, *with the sea behind them, and Astracan as a port of supply within two days' sail of a fair wind, a force might be set down on the eastern shore of the Caspian Sea, either at Balkan, or at Mahgushluc, that with common management might not only capture, but retain possession of Khiva, and* PROJECT AND PREPARE FOR ULTERIOR GREATER ENTERPRISES."—Appendix, p. 69. *Frazer.*

Again:—

"*The great anxiety which the Russians have evinced* to establish a secure footing at *Mangushluc*, and to entertain relations with KHIVA and BOKHARA, will be adverted to in the sequel of this work, and particularly in the geographical notices already alluded to; and *there can be little doubt* entertained by those who have considered the policy of that ambitious state, *that some enterprise* like the above *has been for a long time in its contemplation.* The facilities it possesses are, doubtless, great: with ASTRACAN for a grand DEPOT, and the CASPIAN behind them, they could easily establish a force at MANGUSHLUC, which is *not more than two or three days' sail from their own shores. The conquest of Khiva, and all Khawresm, I do not think would be a matter of great difficulty,* if their attention was once seriously turned that way; and *thus the navigation of the* OXUS *would be in their power.* Wood is to be found, for the purpose of constructing boats, upon the banks of that river, or *it would not be very difficult to transport boats, framed and ready for putting together, from Astracan.*"—*Frazer.*

"It is by no means intended to represent this route as divested of very serious difficulty; all that is meant is to shew that, if the Russian government should think of engaging in such an enterprise, they would, by adopting this mode, SAVE THEMSELVES UPWARDS OF A THOUSAND MILES OF LAND JOURNEY, THROUGH A VERY ILL-FURNISHED OR DESERT COUNTRY, AND ENJOY THE BENEFIT OF WATER-CARRIAGE TO WITHIN ABOUT TWO HUNDRED AND FIFTY MILES OF CAUBUL; and, instead of engaging in the conciliation or conquest of numberless and faithless tribes, they would have only to subdue two insulated sovereigns (Khiva and Bokhara), of very limited powers, and overawe the scattered population of a few hundred miles. What they might have to contend with, after reaching Caubul*, is another question, on which various opinions may be entertained." . . . . . . "Be that as it may, it appears to be the duty of a traveller to point out such localities as he may have seen, and to record such impressions as may have been suggested by them, LEAVING HIGHER AUTHORITIES TO JUDGE OF THE DANGER, AND TO TAKE SUCH PRECAUTIONS AGAINST IT AS TO THEM MAY SEEM EXPEDIENT."—*Frazer*.

Colonel Meyendorf. In 1819, 20, the affairs of France being settled, and the Russian army of occupation withdrawn, the force along the Pruth began to be augmented, the Greek insurrection † broke out within the

* "The conduct of the Douraunies (the feudal princes of Caubul), in their civil wars (says Mr. Elphinstone), gives a very mean idea of their military character. Their armies are very small, seldom exceeding ten thousand men on a side, and these are generally ill-paid and disobedient. The victory is decided by some Chief's going over to the enemy; on which the greater part of the army either follows his example or takes to flight."—p. 538.—"The Cashmerians are of no account as soldiers, and the Afghauns and Kuzzilbasches are enervated by the life they lead."

† Under the conduct of two general officers in the service of Russia—Greeks by birth—one of them aide-de-camp to the Emperor Alexander. It is true, that when Ypsylanty was thrown into prison in Austria, his conduct was censured by the Russian ministers, and he was left to

Principalities, and a new activity seems to have been given to the diplomatic relations of Russia with the East. Missions were almost simultaneously despatched to Bokhara *, to Pekin, to Khiva, the Toorkomauns,—previously to Khokand.

---

his fate; but this will not be considered a conclusive proof, one way or the other, as to who were the real instigators of the insurrection.

* Bokhara adjoins Caubul. There are three principal people or states intervening between the Indus and the Eastern shore of the Caspian—the *Khivians*, Bokharians, and Afghauns of Caubul. To the latter (Caubul) we, as will be remembered, sent a mission at an earlier period—that of Mr. Elphinstone, late governor of Bombay. In going to their destination, the Embassy proceeded by a circuitous route to the southward, through the desert of Bikaneer, Moultan, &c. In passing this desert, a considerable number of the native followers were attacked with slow fever and died. They returned by Attock, the Punjaub, the British cantonment of Loodeana—being the line usually followed, or pretty nearly so, by invading armies. The country was tolerably cultivated, numerous towns and good villages were met with, and no difficulties or losses spoken of.—Several years previously, the Russians appear to have anticipated the probability of our sending an embassy to Caubul. "*The friendship of the Abdalli* (of Caubul) *may be of consequence to the English to cultivate, as the most* EFFECTUAL CHECK *on those who pass* THROUGH BOKHARA TO INVADE INDIA." (1800.) *From an original paper, quoted by Eton.*

Colonel the Baron Meyendorf accompanied the mission to Bokhara, being charged with the statistical branch of inquiry, and has since published the result (1826). With respect to the objects of the mission, and on military topics, this officer is reserved*. On matters of general information and science, his remarks have been

---

* The escort consisted of about five hundred infantry and cavalry; two pieces of cannon; two boats, carried on carriages, for the construction of a raft or bridge; twenty-five three horse waggons, for those who might fall sick; and fifteen felt tents or huts. As, owing to unforeseen delays, it became the depth of winter before the mission set out, two months provisions of biscuit, corn, and spirits were conveyed upon three hundred and twenty camels; thirty-eight camels carried the presents and private baggage; about three hundred and forty camels, belonging to Bokharian merchants, accompanied the party; one hundred and five pounds of biscuit for each man, and four quintals of corn for each horse, was the calculated supply. A Khirghiz Khaun, with some hundred cavalry, desirous of recommending himself to the Czar, solicited the honour of attending the Ambassador for some hundred miles of the journey, which was accepted. There were four hundred sumpter or saddle horses. The sands were so heavy at one time, that many of the draft horses died; but none of the other horses were lost *during the march* (il ne mourut pas un seul cheval de selle). There must have been altogether

highly approved. There are, however, a few passages in the work bearing on the present case.

" The progressive advance (he says) of knowledge in Russia, calls upon that vast empire to realize this generous idea. It is to Russia that the office belongs, of imparting to the Khanats of Central Asia a salutary impulsion, and of diffusing throughout those countries all the benefits of European civilization."—p. 303. *Meyendorf.*

In order, however, to effect this beneficent purpose, the usual process, we find, from the Baron, had best be adopted by Russia—namely, that of

---

scarcely under a thousand persons, as many horses, and seven hundred camels.

But the line of march of this mission over the Desert to Bokhara has no reference whatever to the route for an army, which forms the subject of this inquiry. A writer in the QUARTERLY, by some inadvertency, it must be presumed, has supposed them the same; and argues, for some pages, under this mistaken impression.

The Russians were remarkably healthy, and the air of all that part of central Asia is mentioned by them as being singularly pure and invigorating.

Though guarded apparently in his expressions, some of his remarks are significant,—for instance, " Beyond Meimaneh, one passes over a mountainous country to *Herat* which offers, however, *practicable roads for artillery.*"—p. 144. Paris edit.

taking possession of a due portion of these countries, which would have the additional advantage, he anticipates, of augmenting the *Russian commerce with Asia.*

"This communication (for the caravans) would be perfectly sure, if the Khanat of Khiva were subjected to Russia."—p. 247 *.

"Independently of a great commercial advantage, the acquisition of this Khanat would have that of diminishing enslavement, and the frightful commerce in human beings, especially Russian subjects, which the Toorkomans and Khirghis carry on; it would also augment the salutary influence of Russia in western Asia.

"It would be (he says) in skirting these mountains (between the Aral and Caspian), at a distance of five, ten, or fifteen versts from the Aral Sea, that Russian troops could approach Khiva most easily!"—p. 104.

The Consul Gamba.

With respect to the views of the Russians, as to the augmentation of their overland commerce with India, the reader is referred to the recently published volumes of the Chevalier Gamba, Consul from France at Tiflis. These may be con-

* Although employed on totally different missions, Colonels Meyendorf and Mouravief are on this point completely in unison.

sidered as their text-book on the subject, and must be admitted to be cleverly written, although breathing throughout a most unusual spirit of hostility to the "*dominators of the sea.*" They contain a great deal of information, besides various projects (*rather too sanguinely indulged in, it may be hoped*) for the extension of the Russian commerce and power in the East—to our detriment. "Khiva," he says, "ought to be taken "possession of by Russia;" and to demonstrate the facility of doing so, he affirms (whether truly I know not) that, about twenty years ago, a party of Cossacks made a marauding excursion from the Oural to Khiva, which they seized on and retained possession of, till the government was made acquainted with the circumstance, and recalled them. There is no doubt that the overland commerce with Bokhara and India is obtaining, since 1821, a great extension. The last *Petersburg Gazette* that I have seen mentions, as an ordinary occurrence, the departure of a caravan from Troitz * to Bokhara, consisting of three

* One of the objects of the Russians who have written on this subject, appears to be to cause the transfer of the chief

thousand six hundred and seventy camels. Half a dozen years back the caravans of a whole year were scarcely more considerable*. A volume was published last year at Berlin, with the same object, and in precisely the same tone of hostility to England, so strongly characteristic of the work of the CONSUL at TEFLIS. Nor does it seem irrelevant to observe, that his Imperial Majesty the Czar has conferred on M. Gamba, in testimony of his satisfaction, a "large grant of land on the Phasis."

It is no doubt in pursuance of these views that so ungracious a prohibitory system has, within the last half dozen years, been adopted by the cabinet of St. Petersburg, to the almost total

---

part of this trade from Troitz and Orenburg, to the port of Krasnovotz, or to the Bay of Balkan, on the eastern shore of the Caspian,—from whence the Chevalier Gamba conceives the transit to Bokhara (by the way of Khiva) would not require a longer time, than from one extremity of France to another. The distance may be about the same.

* "Une caravane va tous les ans de Boukhara en Russie, et de la Russie à Boukhara ; elles sont composées d'environ cinq mille chameaux."—1813. *Meer Izzet Ulla; Mr. Moorcroft's Moonshee.*

exclusion of Indian produce previously carried thither on English bottoms.

In 1819, 1820, Colonel Mouravief*, of the Staff of the Russian Guards, was employed on a mission to Khiva. Having since published an account of his journey, the following is an extract from it:— *Colonel Mouravief.*

"The climate and soil, however, of Khiva are favourable to the culture of many of the useful products of temperate regions. If this country were under the government of Russia, it would certainly animate and promote industry, and procure great advantages to our commerce; all that of the higher Asia, and even of India, would then be able to pass by the way of Khiva, and thence to Astrakhan. Already caravans, coming from more southern countries, arrive at Khiva: if this commerce has not acquired more extension, it is because of the interruptions it is subject to by being frequently plundered by the Nomade people. *If we possessed Khiva, of which the conquest would not be*

---

* The same who is spoken of by Mr. Frazer.—"Although (says the above work) the sources of the commerce of Russia with Asia cannot be compared with those from whence such torrents of wealth are poured into Great Britain from India, still the opportunities which are open to *us* might, in time, be made to acquire a sufficient importance to diminish the monopoly (of England)."

difficult, the Nomades of Central Asia would dread our power, and a commercial route would be established from the Indus and Oxus (or Amou) even into Russia; then would all the treasures of Asia enrich our country, and we should see realized the brilliant project of Peter the Great: MASTERS OF KHIVA, MANY OTHER STATES WOULD BE BROUGHT UNDER OUR DEPENDENCE. In a word, Khiva is, at this moment, an advanced post, which opposes itself to the commerce of Russia with Bokhara and Northern India; under our dependence, Khiva would become a safeguard, which would defend this commerce against the attacks of the dispersed people in the Steppes of Central Asia. This oasis, situated in the midst of an ocean of sand, would become the point of reunion for all the commerce of Asia, AND WOULD SHAKE TO THE CENTRE OF INDIA THE ENORMOUS COMMERCIAL SUPERIORITY OF THE DOMINATORS OF THE SEA *."

The fact, it may be conjectured, is, that those who ridicule the idea of danger from Russia, are persons who have long been accustomed to look to France in all their speculations; and,

---

* The route from Khiva to Astrakhan might, it is stated, be greatly shortened, since it is only seventeen days' march from Ourghendj to Krasnovodsk (on the bay of Balkan), from whence, with a fair wind, one may go in a few days to Astrakhan. From the other port,—Manghusbluc,—it appears that, with a fair wind, the voyage to Astrakhan is usually no more than twenty-four hours.

having made up their minds that France cannot attack our Indian empire, they save themselves the trouble of thinking, and apply the same reasoning to this new Power, merely substituting in their minds the word "Russia" for "France." For my part, I cannot see why we should have made such exertions to get the French out of Egypt, if we are to be indifferent respecting the movements of Russia.

Again, at page 333, the Russian Envoy dwells on the same idea :—

"At present (he says), in spite of every obstacle, the external commerce is very advantageous to the *Khivians;* but it would be quite of another description *if the country was subjected to a wise government.* These regions would, in that case, arrive at a high degree of splendour, and all the commerce of the East and of India would direct itself to the northwestern shores of the Caspian Sea; finally, the valuable products of Asia would thus pass by the way of Russia, towards the west. THIS THOUGHT OPENS A VAST FIELD TO THE IMAGINATION! I will return to it, in describing the actual state of Khiva."

"In the present time (says Colonel Mouravief), with the knowledge which we have of the localities of the country, one might guarantee the success of such an enterprise (that of taking possession of Khiva). A CORPS OF THREE THOUSAND RUSSIANS, commanded by a determined and disinterested chief, would be sufficient to conquer and preserve this country, which would be so advantageous to Russia, by reason of the importance of its commercial relations with Asia. We are now in a condition to profit by the information we have acquired of this country,—of the personages who occupy the first posts in the government of Khiva,—of the secret disaffection of the Oosbeks to the Khaun Mohamed-Rahim,—and of the favourable disposition of the Toorcomans with regard to us. The attachment of the latter to Khiva only consists in their drawing their provisions from thence. In furnishing them (the Toorcomans) with grain, which it will be much more advantageous for them to derive from us than from Khiva, we shall easily make them embrace our cause.—AT KHIVA EVEN, WE CAN AUGMENT OUR TROOPS, BY RECRUITING THE THREE THOUSAND RUSSIAN SLAVES * WHICH ARE NOW THERE, AND THE THIRTY THOUSAND PERSIAN SLAVES, WHO SUFFER, QUITE AS IMPATIENTLY

---

* In another place he says,—" When setting out, I was going to load my gun; one of the barrels would not let the air pass when I blew into it; I ordered it to be cleaned, and a paper, rolled up, was taken out. I opened it when I was alone, and read as follows:

" 'Most noble Sir, we take the liberty to inform you, that there are in this country three thousand Russian prisoners, who have to endure hunger, cold, and the insupportable labour imposed on them, as well as all kinds of insults. Take pity on our unhappy situation, and lay it before His Majesty the emperor. Give a poor prisoner cause eternally to pray to God for you.'

" It would be difficult to describe what I felt in reading this note."

AS THE RUSSIANS, THE MISERIES THEY AT PRESENT HAVE TO ENDURE. The only thing which appears to present some difficulty in the execution of this enterprise, is the passage of the steppe which surrounds Khiva; but this may be surmounted with great ease. We are now well-enough acquainted with the route from the borders of the Caspian to Khiva; and as for PROVISIONS—should it be asked, where these are to be procured?—I answer, AT KHIVA ITSELF, WHERE THEY ABOUND. For the means of transport, we can make use of the camels of Toorcomans who inhabit the coast of the Caspian Sea, and who will anxiously press forward, no doubt, to second us*; we can also procure horses from them that are habituated to the Steppes. For the rest, it is enough to remember, that as Mohamed-Rahim penetrated (in 1813) to the shore of the Caspian with twenty thousand cavalry,—so we may feel assured of the possibility of arriving at Khiva with a less numerous corps of infantry, by previously making all the arrangements that might be necessary."—p. 357, 8.

It was in conformity with the opinions so concurrent throughout the foregoing extracts, that the

---

* In corroboration of which, Meyendorf observes, "Les Turcomans qui habitent les côtes orientales de la mer Caspienne, sont en relation avec la Russie ; ils tirent de la farine de ce pays. Presque tous ennemis acharnés des Persans, ils envoyèrent, en 1813, une députation au général Ritchev, pour le prier de ne pas conclure une paix séparée avec les Persans, espérant, disaient-ils, remporter sous peu des victoires signalées sur l'ennemi commun."

author of this publication ventured last year to submit the following propositions:—namely, That, should a war, under existing circumstances, break out between Russia and England, a movement would probably be made by the troops of the former along the "VALLEY OF THE OXUS, AND "THROUGH THE BEAUTIFUL AND FERTILE COUNTRIES "OF BALK AND BOKHARA," against the north-western frontier of British India. And previously also, at pages 18, 19*, these suggestions occur—Whether—IF SUFFERED *to proceed in her career, and to arrange,* WITHOUT OBSTRUCTION, *her materials of operation,*—this power (Russia) may not shortly acquire a degree of intercourse with India that will enable her—first, to disturb and disaffect the public mind of that country towards us; secondly, to move (say 30,000 men, exclusive of the maintenance of communications) from the *Caspian* † and *Aral* as a base, and by

* "Designs of Russia."

† The Russians being the only navigators of this sea, and having no enemy to combat on it, have greatly reduced their marine force on the Caspian. But if it should become useful to form an armament there, there are few dockyards

the Oxus as a principal line of communication, to the neighbourhood of Attock on the Indus, or into the Punjab,—there, perhaps, to take post during a period as a rallying point for the disaffected, or as a beacon for their encouragement and direction;—whereby India must soon become either untenable to us, or, from the excess of expenditure over receipts, resulting from this state of things, unworthy of further retention.

The above can of course add no weight to what has been already transcribed from so many better sources to the same effect; and are here brought forward merely to show that the suggestions on this point, in the Essay alluded to, were *not* adduced without the support of numerous and ample authorities.

---

in Europe in which it could be done with greater facility or less expense than at *Astrakan.—Gamba.* In 1820 steamboats have begun to be constructed on the Wolga: we find, from the same writer, that there can be no difficulty in extending their use from that river to the Caspian sea. Round Azof there are immense fields of coals—in many places almost on the surface.

Thus, then, we find that the governments of England, France, Russia, and of the East India Company, have at various times acted under the impression that an attack by an European army against the frontier of the Indus was not an impracticable enterprise. And this, too, though it were even to commence from the Caucasus, the Euphrates, the Levant, or the Nile—points of departure from at least one to two thousand miles more distant from our northern provinces than the base so constantly assumed for the Russian operations in the preceding extracts—namely, the eastern shore * of the Caspian: devoid likewise of the incalculable facility afforded in the latter and lesser route, of a navigable river flowing directly along the supposed line of advance.

Nor is it undeserving consideration, that the whole body of the inhabitants of Hindostan, Native and English, civilian as well as military, are persuaded of the probability of this event.

* The ports of Balkan and Mangushluck.

Their fate and interests are peculiarly involved; and they possess an advantage over us of this hemisphere, towards a correct judgment—that of being at least ten thousand miles nearer (or rather being close upon) the anticipated field of action.

The preparation for this undertaking, by the line of the Oxus, stated to have been ordered by Catherine, was put a stop to by her death. Under Paul, by his assassination.

Napoleon's line of march, or that of the Russians, through *Persia or Asia Minor*, would, even if supported by the Turks, have been seriously exposed on the right flank and rear to descents and enterprises from our fleet along the Persian shore, in the Gulf and the Levant. To what kind of disturbance would the navigable line that has been pointed out be liable? It is to be apprehended, *none* of any consequence. Certainly it is beyond our reach. The Persians would be the only people of any military power within a thousand miles of either flank of it. Between the Persians on the one hand, and the Toorkomanians, Khivians, and Bokharians on the other, an irreconcileable hatred exists*, founded in virulent religious antipathy, mutually perpetuated by atrocious petty hostilities. The Toorkomanians have even sent a deputation to Georgia, to beseech the protection of the Emperor, and that he might deign to cast an eye of pity ("*regard miséricordieux*") on their situation †. The Persians were enabled to procure the rejection of this entreaty. How long the latter may be in a condition to obtain this complaisance at the hands of Russia, it is not difficult to divine.

---

* Nor is there any greater probability of an alliance between the Khivians and Bokharians.

For some ages past, an almost constant hostility has subsisted between these two countries. Khiva has been conquered several times, and has always recovered its liberty. Emir Haider possessed himself of it ten years ago. This superstitious prince allowed it to resume its independence, in order to conform himself to a precept of the Koran, which forbids a Mussulman to retain possession of the property of those of his faith. Recently, again, the pillage of a great many caravans by the Khivians has caused a misunderstanding between the two khanats. It appears, by some late Petersburg gazettes, that they are now actually engaged in hostilities. Their war appears to consist in surprising caravans, and laying waste villages.

† From the same writer (p. 227) we find that another petition has been sent to the governor of Astrakan, praying, in the name of all the Toorkoman nation, that they may be received under the domination of the Russian government.

It even appears likely that the Persians may be induced to send a force towards Caubul, to co-operate with the Russians, and share in the anticipated booty of Hindostan. A court and people so corrupt, venal, and avaricious, could hardly resist the baits that may so easily in this case be held out to it. Resist, however, they probably could not, at least with any effect, as affairs now are. The army of the Araxes is, since the recent war, in possession of the passes that were supposed to cover Teheraun. This circumstance, the utter exclusion from the navigation of the Caspian, the inefficient military means of the Shah, and the distracted state of the country with reference to the succession, place, it is now but too generally feared, the Persian monarchy at the mercy of the Autocrat. Some twenty or thirty scions of the reigning dynasty, or of rival houses, aspire, it is imagined, to independence or the throne. Thus their wily adversaries have an ample field in which to sow dissension. The consequences are obvious.

Of the other means of resistance which can alone be contemplated to the progress of the

Russians—namely, on the part of the three states or nations lying along their line of march, (the Khivians, Bokharians, and Afghauns of Caubul,) should they be disposed to resist, the opinions of those who may have respectively visited these countries will be briefly adduced.

ON THE

DEGREE OF MILITARY RESISTANCE

TO BE CALCULATED ON,

IN ADVANCING THE RUSSIAN BOUNDARY ALONG THE OXUS RIVER,

THE SUPPOSED LINE OF APPROACH TO INDIA.

THE inhabitants of the tracts comprised in this enquiry, are no longer that great and powerful people which produced a Ghengis and a Timour, the conquerors of Asia, whose posterity were seen seated on the most splendid throne in the world. It is now received, as a general position of history*, that those immense bodies of soldiers which spread over and ultimately subdued the dominion of Rome, under the names of Goths and Vandals, were the Tartars of Bokhara, Khiva, and the shores of the Caspian. The khaun of Bokhara may be considered as the chief, or at

---

* Foster.

least the superior, of those of the Tartarian or Toorkoman states; but his power is of a very limited order. The tribes of the more eastern regions, from whence went forth the conquerors of China, are no longer a cause of dread to any nation of Asia, and are even themselves in great awe of the Chinese, who frequently chastise them, on account of their predatory incursions, in a most sanguinary and merciless manner.

These last are the descendants of the warlike Scythians, who repelled the elder Cyrus from the celebrated Jaxartes (the modern *Sir*,) and who combated with such constancy, and, though not with success, with glory, against the Macedonian Greeks, led on by the *mighty murderer*—Alexander, as he was not very inaptly styled, by the Brahmins.

During the three years anterior to the passage of the Indus, *Balk* (Bactria) was usually Alexander's head-quarters. It was in these countries that he experienced his only serious reverses in the field.

While the Greeks were founding and fortifying Alexandria, a limitary town (somewhere near the present Khokand), which was named by the Greeks *Eschata* or *Extreme**,—the *Bokharians* (ancient *Bazarians* or *Sogdians*) rose to insurrection in their rear, under the Persian nobleman Spitamenes. They got possession of the royal city of Sogd, and marched forward to Samarcand (ancient Maracanda), of which city they also possessed themselves, laying siege at the same time to the Macedonian garrison in the citadel.

Alexander, not deeming the matter of sufficient moment to require his presence, detached a reinforcement to Samarcand of 2400 Greek mercenaries. Spitamenes was compelled to raise the siege, and fall back on Bokhara. Thence the Greeks pursued him with a division of about 5000 men into the Steppes, in the direction of Khiva.

Spitamenes was now reinforced by some of the Toorkoman, or Nomade people, and attacked, in turn, his pursuers. Some misunderstanding prevailed among the Macedonian generals, partly owing to which, a total defeat was sustained; only 300 infantry and 40 cavalry got back to Samar-

---

* Williams.

cand, the citadel of which was re-invested by Spitamenes.

Alexander no sooner gained intelligence of this disaster, than he hastened in person, with a chosen body of troops, to the relief of Samarcand, and accomplished, by forced marches, ninety miles on the fourth morning. The enemy retired again over the same ground as before, followed by Alexander. It does not seem ascertained that any very decided success attended this operation. He passed over the field of the recent defeat, buried with due honours the slain, and, turning his wrath against the inhabitants, laid waste a considerable part of the country.

The Sogdians, or Bokharians, remained in arms, but evaded coming to action, and Alexander retired, towards the end of the season, across the Oxus, and spent the winter at Balk.

It was in the course of this winter, that, during a midnight carousal at the last named place, the unhappy broil took place which terminated in the murder or death, by the hand of Alexander,—of Clitus.

About this time also, Pharasmanes, king of the

Khivians (Chorasmians), came to Balk, escorted by 1500 cavalry, to pay his respects to the conqueror of Asia, and to offer his services in guiding and provisioning the army, if Alexander wished to subdue the nations to the north and west of the Caspian Sea. Pharasmanes was treated with due consideration, and told to place himself in communication with Artabazus, Satrap of Bactria *.

For two years, *Spitamenes* maintained the war with astonishing spirit and activity. At length, some of the barbarians who had joined him, being defeated and driven to despair, put him to death, and sent his head to Alexander. Had he survived, it seems almost doubtful what his ability, fortitude, and perseverance might not have effected.

Alexander was twice wounded during these harassing operations at Bazaria (Bokhara or Sogd), and at the siege of Cyropolis. His marriage eventually with the beautiful Roxana, the daughter of one of the petty princes of Balk, tended greatly to

---

* "Had Alexander known of its proximity (that of Khiva) to the Sogd (Bokhara), he would, in all probability, have paid it a visit."—*Williams.*

reconcile the people, who considered this a compliment to the Bactrians generally.

At length, matters being settled, and tranquillity established, Amintas, with 13,500 men, was left as Governor of the whole region between the Sir, either bank of the Oxus and the Hindoo Coosh.

The whole army, considerably above 100,000 strong, now assembled at Balk, and commenced, in the beginning of summer, its march to the Indus. Ten days were occupied in surmounting the Hindoo Coosh range of hills. Thus were waged Alexander's arduous and toilsome sixth, seventh, and eighth campaigns, amidst the remote, but (as his historians paint them) *delightful* regions of Tartary; and contending, with various success, against the bravest antagonists whom the Macedonians had had to encounter.

How fallen the natives of these countries now are, in strength of character and national spirit, will be best exemplified by the following details.

Military Force of Khiva.

The army which the Khaun (of Khiva*) is in a

* It was in the Khanat of Khiva that Tamerlane first raised the standard of revolt against the Oosbek oppressors

condition to raise, does not exceed 12,000 men, completely armed. When some imminent danger menaces the country, the army may become more than doubled numerically, but it is not in reality the stronger; because this additional multitude, having neither any taste for a military life, nor any knowledge of the use of arms, presents only an ill-equipped mass, more embarrassing than useful.

The Khivians have no permanent or standing army. In time of war it consists of Toorkomans and Oosbeks, all totally without subordination and without discipline.*

"As the Khivian army has no infantry in it, it can *only* combat on the plain, and cannot give an assault to *Colonel Mouravief.*

---

of Samarcand. His great but devastating predecessor, Ghengis, laid waste this Khanat with fire and sword. About eighty or ninety years ago, the Persian monarch, Nadir Shah, (on his return from India,) marched from Bokhara upon Khiva, plundered and demolished that city, and destroyed the Khaun, his two brothers, and several others, by burying them alive in the earth.

* And of whom "thousands (this officer conceives) would be seen to fly before one hundred men of a regular army."

any place that is in the slightest degree fortified. If, sometimes, they dismount to make an attack of this sort, it is only when some imperious circumstance compels them to it*.

"Every soldier is obliged to lay in provisions for the whole period of the campaign; so that every trooper who is at all at his ease in circumstances, carries with him a camel laden with provisions†: the poorer sort of persons have usually one camel between two. One may thus form an idea of the incumbrances of a Khivian army, and of the number of servants and slaves which must accompany it; and, finally, of the difficulty and embarrassments of effecting a *levée en masse*, having with it so considerable a baggage. This is the reason why a Khivian army never makes, and can never make, above thirty werstes (about twenty miles) per day: it even makes less than this progress when it pillages, which it usually does, the country through which it passes.

"An army of this kind cannot keep the field more than a month and a half; and, in short, not being inscribed on any muster-rolls, regularly kept, and receiving no pay, separates when it pleases, and nobody is exposed to the least pursuit or punishment.

---

* They have no pistols—and from their exceeding slowness and want of address in the management of fire-arms, their matches, we are told, very often go out, before they apply them to the priming. Their bows and arrows are small and weak.

† From this also may be inferred the great abundance of beasts of burden.

" Whoever has seen these Asiatic troops, is aware how small a number of men would be necessary, and how little difficulty there would be in destroying them, or rather in dispersing them.

" The *Russian infantry,* which spreads fear and terror amidst the ranks of Asiatic troops generally, and which even obtains an easy victory over the forces of a civilized state like Persia, certainly would disperse, in a moment, the Khivians, who are far from possessing the valour of the Persians. The order, the silence, and the calm approach of our columns, covered by some 'tirailleurs,' would repulse bodies of men ten times more numerous than ours, afraid as they are of coming to within range of musket fire, and animated only by despair, which the Easterns decorate with the name of valour.

" Their cannon are long, heavy, of small calibre: they do not attempt to use them except in ambuscades, because, on account of their length, they cannot fire them without placing them on a rest*."

" The five principal towns are equally enclosed by walls, and regarded by the Khivians as strong places. These walls are constructed irregularly; they are o a thickness of about twenty feet at their base, three feet broad at the top, and about twenty-five feet high, and

* He could only discover seven pieces of artillery, and these in a wretched state—carriages and wheels broken, &c. When in the field, they are drawn by horses, and the management of them entirely confided to Russian slaves, who, though they know but little about the matter, the Oosbeks consider as not so incapable as themselves.

consist of a mixture of potter's clay and common earth; they are devoid of exterior works, and are totally unprovided with artillery.

"These walls crumble down sometimes; nevertheless, they perfectly fulfil their object, for the Toorkomans and Khirghis fancy they behold in them impregnable fortresses.

"These earthen edifices or fortifications are not provided with a ditch, and can only defend the inhabitants against a small number of cowardly brigands, who happen not to have got at their disposal a ladder. Besides which, if they had one, they would not dare to make use of it for entering a building surrounded by a wall, because they would then fall into the hands of their enemies without their horses, and without the means of rapidly effecting their retreat."

"A FORT OF THIS SORT COULD NOT HOLD OUT FOR ABOVE A COUPLE OF HOURS AGAINST FIFTY RUSSIAN FOOT SOLDIERS. SO SOON AS WE SHOULD HAVE REDUCED A FEW OF THEM, THEY WOULD NO LONGER DARE TO HOLD OUT EVEN AGAINST A HANDFUL OF MEN."—*Mouravief*.

MILITARY MEANS AND CHARACTER OF THE BOKHARIANS.

SUCH is the military condition of the Khivians, who are yet dreaded by all their neighbours as the most warlike people of Tartary. The Bokharians are, by their wealth and numbers, considered the most powerful, but individually, on account of their supposed effeminacy and extreme devotion to commerce, they are looked upon with contempt. They are, however, by many degrees more civilised.

Military Force of Bokhara.

The same description of the state of the military art at Khiva will answer for Bokhara, with this difference, that the force may be three times as numerous: but it is even yet less warlike. They are mounted on beautiful horses, and can skirmish, but that is all. Their present king is a harmless bigot, and a pusillanimous devotee.

By the walls of brick dried in the sun, which are described to surround their villages and principal towns, it appears that their notions on fortification are precisely on a par with those of the Khivians.

"Bucharian foot-soldiers, under arms, were drawn up on each side—they made a singular appearance, being men of different ages, old and young, dressed in robes of different colours; some had caps, others turbans, or only drawers; some had boots, others none—all held their matchlocks in both hands. They have but two words of command, 'Rise,' and 'Sit down;' they never pronounce the word 'Fire!' because the matchlocks cannot fire, and because the Bucharians have in fact no infantry. Before our arrival, the Khan had caused all the matchlocks to be collected; they got together 200; and the Khan desired all persons to announce themselves who desired to hold a matchlock, when the Russian embassy should come to visit him. Thus was formed this terrible Bucharian infantry, through which our procession passed to wait upon the Vizier.*

"The road from Kagatan to Basartche being continually intersected by canals, it cost much trouble to get the artillery over the wretched bridges which serve to cross them."

Baron Meyendorf estimates the number of *Persian* slaves at Bokhara at 40,000†: 25,000

---

* Jakovlew.

* By another estimate 60,000 is the number given. Bokhara is surrounded with a clay wall, fifteen or twenty feet high, without outworks, without cannon, and similar to the walls of the Khivian towns.

Khorasan-Persians were lately brought away at once into captivity, from the disaffected dependency of Mawri. There are here slaves of all countries. Most Bokharian gentlemen, of any wealth, have at least forty—persons of rank, even as many as one hundred slaves. To have a large number is considered honourable. They are employed in agriculture. The market price of slaves (of a robust health and strength) is about forty or fifty tellas (twenty-five to thirty-five pounds sterling); but for a good artisan, a carpenter, or blacksmith, as much as £70. The treatment of slaves at Bokhara is described as quite horrible; the Russians complain piteously of being badly fed and beaten unmercifully *."

Their artillery consists of ten Persian guns, of which only three or four are mounted on carriages. These carriages have three wheels, and cannot be moved but with the greatest difficulty†. In a

* "Est-il nécessaire d'avoir vue ces malheureux esclaves russes de Boukhara et de Khiva, pour être animé du désir le plus ardent de les délivrer ?"—*Meyendorf.*

† The ordnance department of *Khokand* is, we may infer, in pretty nearly the same state.—" Before the residence

word, they do no honour to the topshi-bachi, or chief of artillery, who is an old Russian soldier.

The nation, generally, is weak, superstitious, and effeminate. There is here nothing of the fervour of the Arab—it is the degeneracy of the papal Italian that is perceivable. There are, in Bokhara, a great number of richly endowed schools and colleges. The prevailing vice of every class—priest, noble, or peasant—is represented to be a mean and shameless avidity for gain; the redeeming virtue, industry, and an universal inclination to commerce.

---

of the Khaun lie five or six cannons, left by Nadir Shah; but they are quite useless for want of the necessary apparatus."—*Khaproth's Timkowski.*

The artillery of Caubul may be presumed to be in about the same state. In 1809, our officers counted only five guns with the king's army, and these in a worse state than any they had ever seen with a native Indian force.

OF CAUBUL, GENERALLY.

ITS RESOURCES, GOVERNMENT, REVENUE, CHARACTER, MILITARY SPIRIT, AND FORCE.

"CAUBUL, in a political light, has always been considered as the gate of India, towards Tartary;* and is a country highly diversified; being made up of mountains, covered with snow; hills of moderate height and easy ascent; rich plains and stately forests, and these enlivened by innumerable streams of water. It produces every article necessary to human life, together with the most delicate fruits and flowers†.

The town of Peshawar, the second city of Caubul, contains 100,000 inhabitants, more than five miles round, the houses generally three stories high, built of brick, the streets narrow.

---

* Rennel.

† The Emperor Bauber, in his admirable Commentaries, says of the climate, "The air is delightful. I do not believe there is another place like Caubul in the world. Samarcand and Tauris are famous for their climate, but they are not to be compared to Caubul," &c.

"The greater part of the plain was highly cultivated, and irrigated by many water-courses and canals. Never was a spot of the same extent better peopled *. From one height, Lieutenant Macartney took the bearings of thirty-two villages, all within a circuit of four miles. The climate was delicious."

The population of the city of Caubul is stated to be 100,000. The revenue, in settled times, is estimated at three millions sterling.

Almost the whole of the regular troops are cavalry. The horses belong to the men. These horses are mostly from Usbeck Tartary, and the Toorkomaun country along the Oxus. They have a corps, said to amount to seven or eight hundred men, mounted on camels, carrying swivels †.

The usual arms are a sword, spear, and matchlock. They have no commissariat. The villages pay a certain sum to the men whom they send to the army. But in excursions towards India, they will serve without pay.

---

* Elphinstone.

† The king had a guard of a few hundred Hindoostanee sepoys, dressed in imitation of our sepoys, but without discipline. There were only one hundred and fifty at most of (irregular) infantry in the fort of Attock.

Their mode of fighting is the same as that of the Oosbeks and Toorkomauns. A chief, with some of the more valiant and ambitious, sally forth and charge, followed by the others, according as the bravery of each individual may prompt him. If the leaders of this onset are not successful, the whole army considers itself beaten; and then every one provides for his own safety in the best way he can. The common rate of marching of a Caubul army is fifteen or sixteen miles a day.

In a political sense, the kingdom of Caubul, as it is called, is in a state of decomposition. Every petty Dooraunee lord sets up for himself; and subordination is totally unknown. For nearly thirty years a species of anarchy has reigned; notwithstanding which, it is asserted, that the condition of the mass of the people has been improving rather than falling off.

But the best proof of the extreme military feebleness of the Afghans is the contemptible character of the Lahore army on the opposite bank of the Indus, by whom they have been put to flight on several late occasions. Runjeet Singh, the prince of this latter country, has also wrested their finest province from the Afghauns—Cashmere, with its commercial capital of nearly two hundred thousand inhabitants. Until a few years back, it formed part of Caubul.

"The force of Runjeet Singh (says Sir John Malcolm) did not, in 1805, exceed 8000 men. His army is now more numerous than it was, but it is composed of materials which have no natural cohesion, and the first serious reverse which it meets will probably cause its dissolution."

It is not, in short, too much to say, that were the whole force of the Afghauns, Bokharians, and Khivians (the states intervening between the Indus and lower Oxus) combined—it could probably make but a sorry fight of it, against so few even as half a dozen Muscovite regiments.

Of the immeasurable superiority, at present, of European troops, a familiar instance will be in every one's recollection. The confederate Mahratta army, routed at Assye, was by far of a more formidable composition than any now at the disposal of any Asiatic prince. It consisted of 10,500 regular infantry, directed by several French officers, 40,000 cavalry, and considerably above 100 guns. What was the force that effected their overthrow?—About 2000 British, and 2500 sepoy troops, unsupported by the fire of artillery, the draught cattle being unable to keep up with the troops. Scindia's army would have made light of the spears and swivels of Afghaunistan, or of the arrows of Tartary.

"When Holkar fled into the Punjaub (says Sir John Malcolm), in 1805, and was pursued by that illustrious British commander, Lord Lake, a complete opportunity was given of observing the actual state of this nation, which was found weak and distracted, in a degree that could hardly be imagined. It was altogether destitute of union. . . . . . (Individually) there is hardly an infamy which this debauched and dissolute race are not accused (and I believe with justice) of committing . . . . . Every village has become an object of dispute; and there are few, if any, in the Punjaub, the rule of which is not contested between brothers or near relations. In such a state, it is obvious, the Sikhs could alone be formidable to the most weak and distracted governments. . . . . . When the British and Mahratta armies entered the Punjaub, they were both daily joined by discontented petty chiefs of the Sikhs, who offered their aid to the power that would put them in possession of a village or a fort, from which, agreeably to their statement, they had been unjustly excluded by a father or a brother."

So, no doubt, would the Russians be joined,

if they presented themselves, by crowds of the same demoralized chieftains.—An army of Cherokees, or of Oteheyteians, would not fail to obtain allies amongst them, on similar terms, and from similar motives. Such a thing as union, patriotism, or national spirit, is unknown in all those countries.

Since writing the above (September 3rd), I accidentally met with the following piece of intelligence, copied from the ST. PETERSBURGH GAZETTE, dated 13th August :—

" MOHAMMED MUSTAPHA, Prince of the Afghans, arrived here, on the 7th, from Orenburg. The Afghans are a warlike, nomade people, on the frontiers of British India, and are able to bring about 20,000 men into the field. Since the year 1826, the country has been governed by two brothers, sons of Timur Khan*, who died on the 7th of May, 1793. One of them, YAR-MOHAMMED, resides at *Peishawar*. The two brothers are known in India as distinguished warriors. A third brother, DOST MOHAMMED KHAN, who resided at CAUBUL, was expelled, in 1826, by these two brothers. The Afghans, as well as their neighbour, the RAJAH of LAHORE, who lately had two ambassadors at *St. Petersburgh*, are known to be friends to Russia."

---

* The same of the imbecility of whose government Foster speaks.

Here we have the Cabinet of St. Petersburgh negotiating at our threshold! What can the Cabinet of St. Petersburgh have to do with the Rajah of the Punjaub, or the petty princes, adventurers, or usurpers, on either bank of the Indus? Reports have, for three or four years, circulated in India of there being a lively interest evinced by the Russians in the affairs of these bordering states, and that promises were held out to some of supporting their pretensions with an armed force. I was unaware of the tangible shape the intercourse had assumed.

The distracted political state of Caubul, and the ambition of the Lahore Court, certainly offer facilities to any scheme of interference which the northern government may be disposed to practise.

But what is called the Lahore army is, in reality, no better than an unpaid rabble of thieves, to be easily dispersed by any regular force that may be sent against them. Not long since, one of their divisions rose in mutiny, and put their Sirdars to death, on account of arrears of pay. This is quite an ordinary occurrence.

Ool Moolk, of Caubul, who reigned in 1808, was

immediately after dethroned, and was subsequently usually living under the protection of Runjeet, who occasionally made use of him as a political engine against the Afghauns. Ool Moolk was supplanted by his half-brother, Mahmood, who had himself previously reigned, and been also deposed by popular insurrection, or by the versatility of the feudal khauns. During his deposition he had fled to Bokhara, thence towards Khiva; from whence, at the time alluded to, he had returned in arms, and met with but a feeble resistance. At an earlier period (1801) Mahmood had raised the standard of revolt against an elder brother, *Zemaun.* Zemaun was, however, if I rightly recollect, put *hors-de-combat* by his fraternal rival having caused his eyes to be put out. Mahmood himself is now also an uncrowned fugitive, somewhere in the neighbourhood of Herat, but still pretending to the recovery of power. In the mean time, there are at present, I believe, several brothers of another family, who have of late alternately divided the Afghaun state amongst them; a scene of general anarchy and confusion being the natural consequence. And thus the country is at the mercy of any one who may have the means of advancing into it with a small body of troops.

It is feared that civil dissensions of a similar degree await Persia. "Of the forty sons of the King (says Colonel Kinneir), there is not one who does not look to the throne; nearly one-half of them are governors of towns and provinces, a system which, although it may add to the immediate security of the father, presents a fearful prospect to his subjects."

The Russians are now in possession of the passes leading to Teheraun. They lately guaranteed the succession of Mir Abbas: if he succeed in reigning through their means, it can only be as their dependant.

A deadly hatred prevails between the Afghauns and Persians. Either would join any one in an attack upon the other.

MEANS OF SUPPLY.

As the Punjaub, Cashmere, Caubul*, Balk, and Bokhara, are countries in which agriculture is known to flourish †, and which possess also a fair proportion of good pasturage, with numerous flocks and herds, it would be superfluous to enter into any proof of the facility of procuring in them ample ‡ subsistence for an army, the commonest arrangements for that purpose being adopted. The only question, it is presumed, that can be raised, is with respect to the Toorkomaun (or Toorkistaun) country, between Bokhara and the Caspian including Khiva.

On this head Mr. Morier states (p. 381)—
"The Toorkomauns are great cultivators of

---

* "Herat is a large and populous city, situated in a fine plain, which produces abundance of fruit and corn. . . . Kandahar is a wealthy and flourishing city, where fruit and provisions are cheap and abundant. . . . Caubul, the capital of the Afghaun empire, is larger than Kandahar, and here provisions may also be procured in considerable quantities. From Caubul to Peshawer is one hundred and eighty miles, and from the latter to Attock is fifty miles."—*Macdonald Kinnier.*

† Very tolerable wine also is to be had in those countries, particularly in Cashmere.

‡ See *Appendix.*

corn; their territory yields immensely; and when a scarcity exists in Khorassan, they supply the deficiency. They are rich in all sorts of cattle, and rear a superb race of horses, which, perhaps, are in more estimation among the Persians than those of Arabia." There is here, probably, some inaccuracy. They do actually bring corn to Khorassan, and other markets; but it would seem, from various accounts, that they are the *carriers,* not in general the growers of it. It is grown chiefly in the Khivian country and *Tekeh;* but the generic term of Turcoman is often equally applied to the natives of Khiva and Tekeh.

The wealth of the Khivians consists not in the possession of objects of luxury, nor in specie, but in a great abundance of the necessaries of life, which suffice for their wants and for the payment of their taxes.

"The exports consist chiefly of corn and slaves."* The caravans of Khiva carry to Orenburg, wheat, raw cotton, silk, &c.†

---

* Mouravief. † Malte-Brun.

Mr. Malthus affirms, that the soil of Tartary is in general of great natural fertility. There are, comparatively, but few genuine deserts. The wide extended plains, without a shrub, which have sometimes received that appellation, and which the Russians call Steppes, are covered with a luxuriant grass, admirably fitted for the pasture of numerous herds and flocks. On this point, there are several corroborative passages in the Russian works before referred to.

"The Turcomans, along the eastern shore of the Caspian," says M. Mouravief, "are an idle and careless people, subsisting on camels' milk and corn, which they buy at Astrabad and *Khiva*.

"Before sunrise, on the 2nd of October, we met," he says, "with a numerous caravan of Turcomans, of the tribe of Sgdyr. It consisted of two hundred men and one thousand camels. As they went along, they were very noisy, laughing and singing, and rejoiced at having left Khiva, and having made advantageous purchases of corn.

"On the 3rd, we met several caravans, with corn, from Khiva, from which we learnt that the khan had just imposed a tax upon the Turcomans of eight francs on every camel which should arrive. The Turcomans refused to submit .... Several caravans fled in consequence," &c.

MEANS OF TRANSPORT.

But the means of transport are, in fact, the means of supply. The difficulty is not generally in collecting supplies. A military force in command of any extent of country, can always provision itself, even throughout a series of years. Spain, in the last war, though a thinly-peopled country, and for so long a period exposed to the spoliation of friends and foes, supported throughout, on an average, about 200,000 French soldiers, to which may be added, guerillas, followers, &c., to the amount of at least 100,000 more.

The borders of Portugal, a poor territory, had been, up to 1813, almost incessantly a theatre of contest. When Lord Wellington marched from it, in that year, upon France, one province alone supplied the troops in meat for more than a month in advance. The cattle for this purpose were collected, within a short space of time, in Tras os Montes. The mouths to be fed, counting Spaniards, were not less than 120,000. When the whole force had been combined within the Spanish frontier, there were, probably, 45,000 horses and mules, public and private. Of the mules, 15,000 belonged to the English Commissariat. As this great force was enabled to *advance, without interruption, for many hundred miles,* along a line swept by a retreating enemy, and which had, from the beginning of the war, been the beaten track and principal highway of invaders and defenders, it will serve to shew how, with proper arrangement and a due proportion of the means of transport, troops may be subsisted under the most unfavourable circumstances, and during the most rapid operations.

The desert passed and repassed by Buonaparte, during the Syrian campaign, (being seventy-five leagues across,) was about fifty miles broader than the steppe between the Caspian Sea and Khiva. The march of Sir David Baird's army from Cosseir to Cairo passed over a similar tract *. Buonaparte does not mention, in the

* Totally desert, and nearly destitute of water for 140 miles. Only twelve men and fifteen horses died in this passage.

works subsequently published under his name, the number of beasts of burden he required on that occasion for the conveyance of water. But no particular difficulties are alluded to. The soldiers, he says, had with them eight thousand asses, which were very useful. These animals are considerably larger and stronger in the East generally, than in Europe. He adverts to the receipt of intelligence of water-bags being prepared, for an intended passage of the desert, by 60,000 Turks.

Camels are truly said to be the Ships of the Desert. They abound in eastern countries, and are far superior, for burden, to all other animals. We are informed of tribes of Arabs, consisting of not above fifteen hundred or two thousand souls, and possessing three or four hundred horses, and as many as fourteen hundred camels. The Bedouins take good care, it has been observed, that their camels shall not be overloaded, in order that the numbers wanted to be hired from them may thus be increased. Mr. Burckhardt mentions a caravan (1814) consisting of not more than four or five thousand persons, including soldiers and servants, and yet which had

15,000 camels. The same writer mentions the having estimated, from a rising ground, the camels of the pilgrimage caravans to Mekka, of that year, at from twenty to twenty-five thousand. This, from the smallness of the number, was considered a decisive proof of the increased expense of the journey, and of an increasing indifference to their religion on the part of the Mahometans.*

Napoleon's personal experience, and the reports of the various officers whom he despatched into Persia, and even up to the confines of India, must have fully informed him on the subject of the means of transport generally to be calculated on in those countries. The following is a passage from his posthumous work :—

" Setting out from Egypt, as from a place of arms, to lead an army of 60,000 men to the Indus ; to excite

---

* Only fifteen piastres are paid for a camel from Cairo to Suez. Mr. Burckhardt mentions having hired two camels, for four days, to Arafat and back again, for three dollars. Four days may be about one hundred miles. This is cheap for the conveyance of fourteen or fifteen cwt. I diverge into these particulars, with reference, in part, to the facilities of trading between Trebisond and Bagdad, which the Russians may now be disposed to open.

the Mahrattas, and oppressed people of those extensive regions, to insurrection; 60,000 men, half Europeans, and half recruits from the burning climates of the equator and tropics, carried by 10,000 horses and 50,000 camels, having with them provisions for fifty or sixty days, and a train of artillery of a hundred and fifty field pieces, with double supplies of ammunition, would have reached the Indus in four months. Since the invention of shipping, the ocean has ceased to be an obstacle; and the desert is no longer an impediment to an army possessed of camels and dromedaries in abundance."

If the execution of this march had merely depended on the collecting of 50,000 camels, there can exist no doubt of the complete feasibility of the enterprise. The line of march from the Caspian to the Indus could not require, however, (considering the intervening space of water-carriage on the Oxus,) so much as an eighth or a tenth part, probably, of the transport requisite for proceeding from the place of arms spoken of by Buonaparte. But the facility of procuring camels and horses, to *almost any number*, would even be far greater along the banks of this noble river *.

* And oxen likewise. In ancient times, also, we may infer that those countries supported numerous herds, since,

Buonaparte's plan, at least so far as he subsequently states it, appears to have been to advance straight to the Indus, with the whole mass of his force, and without halting, to create depôts. This, of course, augments the difficulty, and would have demanded vast additional means. But there is a great difference between difficulty and impossibility. What has been done, or nearly so, may, it must be admitted, be done again; although, from other causes, it may have been extremely improbable. Alexander moved, in one campaign, over about two thousand miles of the same ground; but Buonaparte's calculation of being enabled to effect it in four months, was probably, under any circumstances, an error as to time. Two great deserts intervened—that near the Euphrates, the other to the eastward of Persia. The whole distance might have been nearly three thousand five hundred miles; to have accomplished which in four months would have required about thirty miles a day, without intermission—a

---

after an action of no great importance, we find the Macedonians enumerating amongst their booty, "two hundred and thirty thousand head of various kinds of cattle."

rate of progress, with all possible aids and no resistance, out of all range of probability.

The project of the Russians appears to be quite of a different description :—to move three or four thousand men over, for the most part, a sterile steppe, deficient in water, but of inconsiderable breadth. There (at Khiva) to be reinforced by further detachments, to facilitate the bringing up of which arrangement could then be easily made, and also to be recruited, both at that place and at Bokhara, from the unfortunate Russians and Persians at present held in captivity. It is at Balk that, in fact, a considerable train of baggage animals would have to be prepared *. The distance to Attock is nearly five hundred miles. But excepting the Hindoo Coosh hills, of ten or fifteen days in the passage, it is generally a peopled and well cultivated country. The merchant-caravans, which constantly cross the Hindoo Coosh, consist chiefly of horses and ponies, being more adapted than the camel for the defile passes. But camels abound on both sides of the mountain.

* In all these countries we do not read of one strong fortress, nor of any thing which could require siege-artillery.

General Smith pursued Ameer Khan in 1805, seven hundred miles, (occupying forty-three days) with the same troops which had before pursued Holkar, under Lord Lake, for five hundred miles*. When our army terminated its march, in that year, near the altars of Alexander, it had in its train, besides a great number of elephants, some thousand camels, and about 90,000 bullocks: 45,000 of these were in the regular pay of the commissariat. The remaining number were Bringary or belonging to grain merchants, following and providing the bazaars of the army on their own account—to whom, of course, every encouragement is always given. A single convoy, moving to the first siege of Burtpore, had above 40,000 bullocks with it. Neither camels nor horses are abundant in India, which is the reason of our armies being obliged to use so many bullocks. A bullock carries less than one third the burden of a camel: but one camel is

* These and other memoranda of the marches of armies, and of the number of baggage animals in their train, are inserted only with the view of affording the civilian reader a relative idea of what is customary or practicable in those matters.

worth a dozen or more than a dozen bullocks—by reason of its greater capability of marching and bearing hardships, and the lesser space it occupies on the line of march. Bullocks frequently cannot keep up with the troops, and easily sink under exertion. This inconvenience a force coming from the native country of the horse would not have to contend with*.

From better regulation, our troops have often made more rapid marches than the native armies. General Wellesley outmarched the Nagpore army†.

The force which pursued the Paishwah during the last Mahratta war marched over a space calculated at 2200 miles, with horse artillery, in seven months.

A numerous class, as well of the Tartars as of the Afghauns and Khorasauns, live by the hire of their camels. Individuals are known to have as many as seven or eight hundred. The hire of the camels used by the Russian mission

* When General Baird's army marched over the desert from Cosseir to Cairo, the guns were drawn by small Indian bullocks which had been embarked in the squadron.

† Blacker.

to Bokhara, was at the rate of £4. 10*s.** each, for a distance of one thousand miles. The ordinary rate is 4*l.* And on returning from Bokhara to the Russian frontier, it is no more than from 1*l.* 12*s.* to 2*l.* per camel. Three camel-loads is rather more than equal to one ton. And this point (the small amount of hire) has, I rather think, escaped the recollection or inquiry of those who have entered into calculations to prove the impossibility of a considerable commerce being carried on with India by caravans.

It is the custom in Toorkomania for a man to purchase his wife,—a certain number of camels, sheep, or cattle, constituting the price. Five camels is a common price for a girl; from fifty

* This includes every sort of charge—the food of the camels, the guides (who are bound to load and unload them)—every thing is defrayed. Thus, the baggage, double supply of ammunition and provisions for two months for about six or seven hundred infantry, cavalry, artillery, officers and followers, were conveyed one thousand miles at a total cost of £1600. The low price of provisions may likewise be augured from the fact, that the total expenditure for the detachment during seven months' absence from the frontier (exclusive of the two months' supply first laid in) was estimated at no more than seventy-two thousand rubles, or about £2900.

to a hundred are often given for a woman who has been married, and is still in the prime of life*. Next to their horses, the most valuable possession of the Toorkomauns is their camels†. The Bucharian horse is known to be of the finest races in the world. In Khohaun, Fergauna, and other provinces, camels are used for the plough; but in the greater part of Toorkistaun, oxen.

In 1806, a census was taken of the Kalmuks, inhabiting the rich pastures on either bank of the lower Wolga, in the neighbourhood of the Caspian; their number was found to be forty thousand, and are stated to have possessed no less than fifty-seven thousand four hundred and sixty-

---

* "It is somewhat singular," says Mr. Frazer, "that, in these bargains, a widow, who has been some years married, bears a far higher price than a young girl."

† Of the neighbourhood of the Indus also, Mr. Elphinstone observes, "The stock consists of bullocks and camels, which last are kept in numerous herds, and are used to carry loads to ride on and even to plough." Mr. Frazer "found that baggage cattle of all sorts, horses, mules, camels, asses, and bullocks are always in plenty, and generally cheaper at Yezd than in other quarters." Again, "The province of Balk is famous for a strong and active breed of horses, which are exported in considerable numbers."—*Elphinstone.*

three camels*; two hundred and thirty one thousand one hundred and six horses; one hun-

* Tooke, in his View of the Russian Empire, observes, "A more remarkable and interesting object invites our attention—the BEASTS OF DRAUGHT AND BURDEN.....Among the Nomadic tribes, the Khalmuks, Khirgises, and Baschkirs possess the greatest numbers of these animals doubly necessary to them.....There are Khalmuks who possess several thousand horses......They are divided into troops by their owners, to each of which is assigned only one stallion, who plays the shepherd as it were over his flock. THE NOBLE HERBAGE OF THE STEPPES IN THESE REGIONS (the banks of the Ural) affords such encouragement to the breeding of horses, that many individuals among the Baschkirs possess from two to four thousand of these animals .....The cattle of the Nomades consists chiefly in horses, as most of their necessaries are supplied by this animal. They obtain from them, not only meat, milk, and cheese, but even spirituous liquor, skins for their clothing, sinews for sewing, &c........As this is the last time (says Mr. Tooke, who quotes from Pallas) that we shall have occasion to speak of the Khirghises, we will here state the proportion in which the several kinds of animals are found among Nomades. A common herdsman keeps not often fewer than thirty to fifty horses, half as many neat cattle, about as many sheep, several camels, and from twenty to fifty goats. Yet there are men, particularly in the middle horde, who possess as many as ten thousand horses, three hundred camels, between three and four thousand head of horned cattle, twenty thousand sheep, and above a thousand goats. The camels thrive in the warm and salt steppes of the Khirghises uncommonly well."

dred and fifty-seven thousand five hundred and sixty-two (bœufs ou vaches) horned cattle; and seven hundred and fifty-four thousand two hundred and fifty-four sheep.

Every Khivian trooper, who is at all at ease in his circumstances, has with him, besides his horse, a camel laden with provisions. The soldiers who are poor have one camel between two. "So that a Khivian army, (says Colonel Mouravief) what with extra horses, camels, slaves, and attendants of all sorts, cannot march more than twenty miles a day, and is more incumbered than a European army, with a battering train in its suite."

In the revenues of the Khaunship of Khiva, we find an estimated item of 800,000 francs per annum, levied on the camels coming in laden or employed in commerce, at the rate of eight francs per camel. There must, therefore, in this one district alone, be one hundred thousand camels liable to the tax*.

* The last caravan from Troitz consisted, as before stated, of 3600 camels. Now, at three camels per ton weight, this caravan conveyed about as much as two of our smaller India ships, of six or seven hundred tons burden. We find

No more, it is presumed, need be said relative to the available supply of animals of transport throughout the tract referred to. It is the last in the world wherein a deficiency of this kind can be reasonably looked to as a barrier to enterprise.

If, then, the authorities we have cited may be relied on, there is ample reason to infer that the Russian Government does probably contemplate advancing a force towards the "MOST VULNERABLE FRONTIER OF OUR INDIAN POSSESSIONS * ;" neither, as it appears, is there any

---

from Meyendorf, that in December and January there are always crowds of return camels at Bokhara, the owners of which, wishing to get back to the north, are willing to be hired at a very low rate—for instance, to the Russian frontier of Troitz (1000 miles) for from 1*l.* 12*s.* to 2*l.* per camel. From these different data I am inclined to think that goods may be sent for about 8*l.* or 10*l.* per ton weight from *Cashmere*, or the north of India, to *Astracan*, by the way of Balk, the Oxus, Khiva, and the Caspian Sea. The above 100,000 camels, which, it appears, enter Khiva annually from the surrounding country, are equal to a commercial fleet of thirty-three sail of the larger Indiamen, of a tonnage of 1000 each.—Quære: can we send goods for 10*l.* a ton from the port of London to Calcutta (18,000 miles)?—I submit this for the consideration of commercial men.

* Sir John Malcolm.

less ground for inferring, that there as yet exists no insurmountable obstacle to the execution of such a project. I have not been able to per suade myself, after a diligent examination, that there is anything in the conformation of the ground, in the length or difficulties of the route, or the power of the intervening states (whether separately or conjointly), to prevent it; nor am I aware that the defeat of any such hostile attempt can rationally, from any quarter, be anticipated, unless from our own timely and adequate precaution.

Ours is a system in which generally received opinion is not without influence. I incline to think there is an incorrect impression prevalent on this subject. I conceive it probable that those who have not only the power to act, but are most competent to form a judgment, have not perhaps been at liberty, from the pressure of other avocations, to apply to the topic sufficiently in detail; and having myself endeavoured to do so, I have thought the present a fitting time for bringing forward the result. The discussion is, indeed, a dry, but not unimportant one.

Of course, if any such views be really enter

tained, the chances in favour of their being carried into execution must be increased in proportion to the increasing strength of the Russian power, and the reputation of its arms, whether in Europe or in Asia.

Nothing has, in fact, been stated in this inquiry, but what has been already pointed out by our own diplomatic agents; to whose published opinions, no doubt, the Russian Cabinet has not been inattentive. But the Russians have not been obliged to depend on the investigations or statements of our officers,—they have employed numerous agents of their own,—and these have spoken still more confidently on the subject. The Government of the Czars is avowedly despotic in all its branches,—but in none more so than the military department. In all countries it is almost out of the nature of things that a diplomatic functionary shall not coincide with the wishes and opinion of his employers:—in Russia, a breath to the contrary no one so situated would ever think of hazarding. Colonel Mouravief, whose representations on the matters in question are so forcible and sanguine, and whose hostility to the "*domi-*

"*nators of the sea*" is so unreservedly reiterated, does not seem to have miscalculated the tone which would be most agreeable to his Government. Reward, not reprehension, has attended his effusions,—considerable professional advancement having been subsequently conferred on him. Baron Meyendorf, though dwelling more upon science than politics, fully coincides with his brother officer. But I do not propose to give any undue weight to the propositions of these official characters,—they only form links of the chain of evidence which I conceive to have been unanswerably adduced.

If Britain were a petty or a feeble state, possibly it might be well to hope for the inaptitude of her foes or rivals; it might then be indiscreet to speculate too curiously into what may be designed or executed against her:—in such case, a tacit resignation to events (involving what they may) were perhaps the more prudent course—solicitude, or openly expressed anxiety, tending possibly to provoke or precipitate attack.

But I believe it cannot be denied that the case is totally otherwise,—that the *nation* was never before so powerful as it now is,—and that all that is required to us is to know from whence attack may originate, in order to prepare the means of hurling it back upon its source, with every circumstance of signal and accumulated discomfiture. It is to us that (as I, for one, most firmly venture to think) belongs, by pre-eminence, the rarest assemblage of the elements of political strength that exist—the proof of which will not fail to be manifest, provided the complexity of our affairs, and their temporary or remedial derangements, are not permitted to delude, unnerve, or subdue that public spirit which has hitherto constituted one of the noblest and not least useful traits of the national character.

Even if our moral force alone, with at least a very moderate physical aid, were heartily brought into play, what terror might not be scattered, even to the head-quarters of those, who would seem even now leaguing themselves against the independence of nations. When Russia (the restorer of liberty in Greece!) thought proper, a few years back, to propel a crusade against liberty in Italy, in Spain, and in Portugal, the British foreign department propounded to Europe and the world a declaration, which will remain as a monument to its honour. A very slight process on our parts, in conformity with and carrying forward the principles therein so well laid down, would very soon, it cannot be doubted, have the effect, if resisted at least, of dashing to pieces even the foundation of those military thrones, to which the voice of mediation and of a just equilibrium are now in vain addressed. Whether at present resolved on or not, events may possibly, at no distant period, bring into action some such course of policy. Our facilities are unnumbered—our government could as soon do as say it.

Nothing more true than that we possess, what so often by foreigners has been made a ground of accusation—a species of ubiquity. If need be, we could touch with a wand of releasement from civil bondage wherever it exists—or wave the torch of confusion to ill-constituted authority over every shore. Nothing so easy, if we please to apply the match, than to give a new form to the whole political condition of the old continent, and assimilate it either to ourselves or to the new world.

There are only a few spots where combustible matter does not abound.—If even national union were given only to Italy, or comparative independence to Spain, which is now governed in a great degree by the glistening of the Bourbon bayonets from beyond the Pyrenees, and by the recollection of the atrocious denunciations of the Holy Alliance,—what a support would even thus be given to the federative system of Europe!—Herein would be a cheap and a philanthropic warfare.

But I return to my subject.—The first quarrel with England, whenever that may happen, would, in all probability, be the signal for commencing the operation that has been traced in the preceding passages; if with no other object than as a weapon* against the stability of the British power. And there can be no doubt but that the mere appearance of a Russian force upon the Eastern shore of the Caspian would alone be calculated to unsettle and disturb, in a most inconvenient manner, the general feeling of

---

* "*To reduce Britain's strength* (as the Marquess of Hastings anticipates) *would be the purpose.*"

the people of India*; the repression of which, without even reference to actual invasion, would be a source, to say the least, of a most onerous expenditure. These, I venture to think, would be amongst the inevitable consequences of our being taken, in this instance, *unprepared.* As yet, so much even as a topographical inquiry into the military features of these countries by competent persons has not been instituted.

The time likely to be occupied by the Russians in these supposed movements might be about as follows: —

Mr. Frazer was informed by several persons, whose reports coincided, and whose statements he considered worthy to be received, that the distance from the Bay of Balcan to Khiva is twelve days' journey for a caravan†: in another place he gives

---

* For the truth of which I appeal—not to those who acquire their knowledge of India in their closets—but to those who have been in the country, and who personally know something of its public mind.

† From Mertvoy to the Aral Sea is only one hundred miles. There are numerous large fishing-boats employed by the natives on that sea. It does appear possible, that

it at ten days. M. Mouravief states the distance from thence to the neighbourhood of Bokhara, for heavily laden boats, at seven days' voyage*. From this point to within two days' march of Balk may be another voyage of four or five days. Here, then, are twenty-five, or suppose we admit it to be thirty-five days' journey for merchants, which we will allow a Russian force a whole campaign to accomplish ; in order that there may be full time for establishing themselves† in Khiva, Bokhara, Samarcand, &c.

---

this line may be found a convenient one, from thence to ascend the Oxus.

* Three days (his informant remarked) for a robber.

† What they would have to do may, perhaps, be thus enumerated :—1. Placing some small citadel-garrisons in some principal towns.—2. Collecting supplies, horses, camels, boats, &c.—3. Arranging the civil government, or deposing or elevating native rulers, as may seem most eligible.—4. Organizing a chosen body of the natives with the assistance of Russian officers.—5. Disciplining the most efficient of the captives, Russian and Persian.—6. Disarming the population of such towns as there may be any reason to suspect.—7. Establishing a police, of which the least efficient of the liberated slaves might form a part, &c. —There is nothing particularly difficult in all this—if, as is represented to be the case, the military forces of the invaded states be incapable of resistance.

Let us then suppose, that early in the following year there are ten or fifteen thousand Russians, with twenty or thirty thousand newly organised troops, assembled between Balk and the ancient *Anderab* at the foot of the mountains; smaller columns being directed towards the passes leading to Peshawer and Cashmere.

From Anderab, through the defiles of the Hindoo Koosh to Caubul, is one hundred miles*. From Caubul to Attock is about two hundred and thirty miles. It is strange if they cannot accomplish this within the second campaign, aided, as there is but too much reason to apprehend they may be, by many of the discontented and unprincipled Afghaun chieftains;—some of whom are even perhaps, at this very time, urging their invitations to this invasion.

Some persons suppose that we could bring our whole force of above 200,000 men to the front line to meet an invader. This is an error. To be

* It was in commencing this march that Alexander caused the private baggage of the army to be burnt, the soldiers being overloaded with booty, according to Plutarch.

enabled to bring to this extreme frontier line any thing approaching to this number, a vast augmentation of our Indian army must previously take place. We should have to provide for the control of a territory of from fifteen hundred to two thousand miles to the rear, containing a conquered, and therefore, it may be conjectured, not over loyal and attached population. Under such circumstances, a very large proportion of the army would be requisite for this duty.

The internal measures of amelioration calculated to promote the further prosperity of these possessions, and to conciliate the attachment, and consolidate our power amongst the people of them, are so soon to undergo a full discussion in Parliament, that nothing need be said here on those momentous points.

I would observe, however, that we have no political agent permanently resident in either of the Afghaun cities, Caubul or Peshawer. This, I should venture to think to be at present quite as necessary, or rather, indeed, a great deal more so than at *Teheraun*. There can be no difficulty in maintaining a diplomatic intercourse, and interchange of friendly offices, with the government, chief or chiefs, (for the time being) *de facto*. It would seem desirable, also, to make an effort towards giving unity and stability to the Caubul state. That this might not be altogether unfeasible, may be deduced from the opinion of our Envoy thither, "that even if we admit the inferiority of the Afghaun institutions to those of the more vigorous governments of other Asiatic countries, we cannot but be struck with the vast superiority of the materials they afford for the construction of a national constitution."

Some of these remarks would undoubtedly apply equally to Lahore. There is no possible degree of political reform, of which either of these states are susceptible, which can afford us the remotest ground of umbrage. It is almost solely with a view to the use that may be made of them as auxiliary to an European force, that, in a military sense, they deserve to be considered. As for the jealousy possibly arising from any interference we may deem it politic to institute towards improving the internal condition of those two states, *that* ought not, I should imagine, to deter us for a moment from any course which might be otherwise essential to adopt.

Asiatics have, in all ages, been familiar with conquest, and with the undisguised display of overt authority, wherever power exists; and the abstinence from it, or what has been termed the "*non-interference plan,*" they have constantly proved incapable of appreciating.

Some sort of agent, of the consular character, might advantageously also be stationed at Bokhara, if for no other purpose than to have due intelligence of what is passing at so extremely important a station.

Caubul, as before observed, has been invariably regarded as the key of India; whether the invader advance from the west or the north, from Candahar or from Balk. The Hindoo Koosh mountains, which *interpose* between the fertile plains of Balk * and the rich valley of Caubul, are the most

* "The vicinity of the town (of Balk) is well cultivated, and corn and provisions are to be procured in abundance."—*Macdonald Kinneir.*

important feature in all this tract. They form a ramification of the Himalehs, extending from thence in a continuous line to the westward. On the line between Balk and Caubul there are several passes, running chiefly along the beds or sides of the mountain rivers. These, in winter, are subject to avalanches, and are at no season good roads *, although constantly in use, both by armies and caravans, from the most ancient to the present times. There is also a pass from Koondooz to Attock, by the way of Peshawer, and from Koondooz to Cashmere. Timour, we find, from his own statement, entered India in three columns†.

---

* Frazer.

† " When Timour first proposed to his Princes and Emirs the invasion of India or Hindostan, he was answered by a murmur of discontent: '*The rivers! and the mountains and deserts! and the soldiers clad in armour! and the elephants, destroyers of men!*' But the displeasure of the Emperor was more dreadful than all these terrors; and his superior reason was convinced that an enterprise of such tremendous aspect was safe and easy in the execution."—*Gibbon.*

"MY DESIGN (says this Cæsar of the East) for reducing the empire of Hindostaun was this,—First, to discover the thoughts of my sons and of my Ameers, I demanded counsel of them.

"And the Prince Mahummud Sooltaun spoke, saying,—'We may subdue Hind: yet Hindostaun hath many ram-

There were 30,000 cavalry previously stationed in Afghaunistan. These were directed upon Moultan. The centre, consisting of 32,000, also of cavalry, passed by the way of Balk, Caubul, and Peshawer, to Attock. The left wing, of 30,000 of the same arm, from Samarcand, in the direction of Cashmere.

It would evidently be desirable that we should

---

parts. First, the rivers; and, secondly, the wildernesses and the forests; and, thirdly, the soldiers clad in armour; and, fourthly, the elephants, destroyers of men.'

"And others of the Ameers pointed out other obstacles and other objections.

"And I had resolved on the conquest of Hindostaun, and I was loth to desist from my resolution.

"And when I sought an omen in the Holy Book, this sacred verse came forth—'*O, Prophet, fight with the infidels and the unbelievers.*' And when the Doctors of the Law explained the meaning of the verse to the Ameers, they hung down their heads, and were silent; and my heart was grieved by their silence.

"And I deliberated with myself concerning the Ameers, who opposed the reduction of Hindostaun, whether I should throw them down from their commands, and give their troops to their Kotuls: but since I myself had exalted them, I sought not to pull them down; and I treated them with kindness; and although they had angered me, yet, as they were unanimous at last, I regarded it not.

"And I called a council a second time, &c."—*Institutes.*

have a complete knowledge of the Hindoo Koosh, and of the passes through it; as a question would most probably arise as to whether it should not be occupied by a detached corps in support of the native bands, in the event of menaced invasion, and of the Afghauns, or chief part of them, being in alliance with us. It, no doubt, offers strong positions, as an advanced line—if held by a force which knew how to defend them. There is a river (the Paumeh), which falls into the Caubul river, westward of Peshawer, along which runs for some distance the road to Koondooz. This would also, perhaps, be occupied. But these are no more than details and conjectures.—The fact of the operation not being locally impracticable, is, I think, demonstrated.

One word will only be added. It was an established and well-known maxim of the Romans to carry their wars, whenever they could do so, into the territory of their enemies. Thus it was, that in order to put a signal termination to the invasion of Italy, they resolved on assailing the source of Hannibal's power in Africa.—The source of the Czar's encroachments in Asia—is in Europe.

ADDENDUM

TO THE

MEMORANDA OF THE MAP.

THE Greeks under Clearchus and Xenophon made an aggregate of two hundred and fifteen marches from Sardis to Trebisond and Cotyora, averaging fifteen miles each march; the distance, according to Rennel, being 3225 miles.

General Paskewitch, who is probably by this time master of Trebisond, marched his corps, in 1815, from Riga to Mayence in ninety-five days—being 1055 miles; under fourteen miles a day.

At present, our advanced cantonment of Loodeana on the Sutledg, is 1268 miles from the chief British depôt, fortress, and sea-port—Calcutta. If the Russians occupied the strong Caubul country, on the right bank of the Indus, they would be about 1000 miles from their sea-port of debarkation, Balcan.

The Afghauns, Tartars, Persians, and Greeks, have repeatedly invaded India, and almost invariably by the way of Attock. Of these, the most celebrated were under Alexander, Mahmoud, Ghengiskhan, Tamerlane, and Nadir Shah. Zemaun of Caubul penetrated some way into the country about thirty years back. It is ninety years since Nadir's invasion. Mahmoud Ghazni made twelve expeditions into India.

"The Indus is formidable, I understand, at several places between Attock and Hyderabad, where it was crossed by Mahmoud of Ghazni."—*Macdonald Kinneir.* Mr. Elphinstone only speaks of one ford above Attock.

With reference to the quantity of baggage-animals, which it is customary to use, and are available, in those countries, a circumstance may be added: — Colonel D'Arcy, of the British artillery, was at one time appointed to assist in organizing the Persian army; and commanded a corps in the field against the Russians, under the Prince Royal, Abbas Mirza. Eleven guns formed part of this division, and besides some hundred mules, there were seven hundred camels appointed to assist in conveying its baggage. This does not appear to have been considered more than an ordinary supply.

Of other rapid marches in the East, may be mentioned the recent ones of General Pritzler's force, with light artillery, in the last Mahratta war, of 346 miles in twenty-five days; and General Lionel Smith's, with a small battering train, 300 miles in twenty-six days.

GENERAL VIEW

OF THE RUSSIAN EMPIRE—ITS EXTENT—EARLIER HISTORY, &c.

THAT part of the history of the Russians which we can trace with any degree of certainty, covers a comparatively very short space of time. It is filled, however, with many great and striking incidents. But, before proceeding to some notice on that head, it will be as well to advert briefly to the extent, boundary, climate, productions, and, in short, actual physical condition of the country.

England, France, and Spain, seem to be surrounded, in some degree, by natural barriers, which have prevented, even during a long course of centuries, any very considerable permanent extension or diminution of their territories. Such, however, does not appear to have been the case with respect to Russia, which, in its origin of *Grand Princedom of Novgorod,* was not of wider extent than either of the kingdoms just mentioned.

Ninety different states, kingdoms, or principalities, compose the Russian empire—occupying, altogether, one-half of Europe, one-third of Asia, and a considerable tract in America; and forty different languages or distinct dialects are said to be spoken within its limits.

The larger portion of Asiatic Russia (Siberia) was conquered no longer ago than the sixteenth century; Russian America (California) was taken possession of in the eighteenth century. But the possessions in Asia and America are only thinly inhabited, and for the most part by poor and barbarous tribes; amongst whom, however, improvement is going on, owing to the establishment of colonies, by means of commerce, and through the protecting care of the Government. The extreme northern part of Siberia is almost throughout a frozen swamp and irreclaimable solitude. But the southern tracts are rich in subterranean treasures, in ores of all kinds, particularly iron and copper. Peter the Great was so anxious to promote the working of the mines, that he wrought in one himself at some sixty miles from Moscow, which now belongs and yields a great revenue to the noble and powerful family of Narishkin. Demidoff is the name of another magnate family, whose immense wealth is derived from mines.

Russia is, from east to west, about 10,000 miles long, and from north to south 2500, being a more spacious dominion than was ever before brought under the sway of any one sceptre or government. The Roman monarchy, at the height of its grandeur, extended, as the reader will recollect, from the Euphrates to the Western ocean, a distance of 3000 miles; while its breadth measured about 2000, from the wall of Antoninus in Scotland to the pillars of Hercules. It, therefore, scarcely equalled in magnitude even the portion of Russia lying within the European frontier.

But, perhaps, it may convey a clearer idea of the size of this lesser division of the empire, by observing, that it is nearly twelve times as large as England, Ireland, and Scotland, together.

But the population is not equally great in proportion,—being only fifty-seven or fifty-eight millions, besides fifty thousand Americans, and two or three millions of Asiatics; while ours, within so much smaller a space, amounts probably to twenty-four millions. Here it may not be out of place to remark, that the number of human beings subject to the King of England is greater than under the sway of the Czars, or of any other Government,—that of China excepted. But, on the other hand, the eighty or ninety millions of Indians who people the British Eastern conquests can scarcely be classed under the head of a national population, such is their detached and remote position; and having been, in fact, neither incorporated nor colonized, they are still held chiefly by the prowess of our fleets and armies, and through the assistance of large bodies of natives; —by means of their own dissensions, and through their inferior knowledge and want of patriotism. Thus it is a country rather in our occupation than an integral part of the empire.—But to return to our subject.

Russia is bounded on the west by Germany, the Baltic, and Sweden; on the south by Turkey, Persia, Tartary, China, the Euxine, Azof and Caspian; on the east by the Pacific, beyond which, however, is California; and on the north by the Frozen Arctic.

Generally speaking, European Russia is a level country; the southern and central parts, particularly those between the Don and the Volga, are of an exuberant fertility, never requiring, we are told, to be manured. It is watered by numerous and important rivers, which traverse it in every direction. Of these, the Duna and the Neva fall into the Baltic; the Ural, the Emba, the Volga into the Caspian; and into the Euxine, the Don, the Dnieper, the Bog, the Dniestre, and the Danube. Most of these are navigable for many hundred miles. The Volga is said to travel four thousand versts in its course, and is navigable for vessels of heavy burden throughout the greater part of that distance. Further, by means of canals, which connect the more contiguous points of the rivers, a complete and most valuable series of water communications has been established throughout the whole empire. The introduction, also, on some of the larger rivers, of the late happy invention—the steam-boat—is said to have given a new impetus to commerce and agriculture*.

The forests are numerous, abounding in timber of every description—in some provinces, beyond the utmost consumption of the people, and requiring eradication ; in others, there is a scarcity of wood, which is a severe detriment, and checks the increase of population. The more extensive forests lie between St. Petersburgh and Moscow, and these seem inexhaustible. The birch and resinous kinds grow in the north ; the oak, and those which are massive and of a durable texture in the middle and meridional parts.

The agricultural produce in general far exceeds the wants of the home markets. What is needed is a free outlet for the surplus.

Salt is produced in amazing quantities. The government reserves to itself the preparation and sale of this article ; and the people are supplied with it on very moderate terms.

There are, in various provinces, numerous herds

* Dupin.

of horned cattle, of which the hides and tallow form a staple article of import into England. Sheep flocks are on the increase, especially in the Ukraine. The Merino breed has been introduced, and thrives. Camels are in great numbers in the southern governments; as are rein-deer in others, which are of great utility as an object of chase, for food, and as a domestic animal for riding, draught, &c.

In the lakes and rivers which intersect and indent, and in the oceans which wash, the shores of the empire, there is no deficiency in the supply of fish for the nourishment and other purposes of the inhabitants: of these may be mentioned the sturgeon of the Volga and Caspian, the whales, the hippopotamus, and porpoises of the North Sea.

The mines of iron and copper have been alluded to; those of silver, gold, and platina are also worked, especially of late, with success. A very handsome platina coin, beautifully executed, has been lately issued by the government, and passes current: it is something larger than our half sovereign, and is valued at ten roubles. Yet there is one sad drawback to this favourable description which must not be forgotten—the great body of the people are in the humiliating condition of vassals, and of course are very imperfectly civilised: the government, too, is a despotism, though by no means an unenlightened or unbenevolent one.

The climates of such a country must be extremely various. The provinces lying towards the south enjoy a warm and agreeable temperature, in which, with a rich soil, all the plants and vegetables of the most favoured countries flourish in superfluity. In the middle and northern regions, the winters are very cold, and there all the products of agriculture are proportionally stinted. But this is only felt, to any considerable degree, in the very high latitudes; where, though not congealed in everlasting frost, the ground is long and severely oppressed by it. Here nature supplies, in part, the deficiency; corn is not dispensed; but for the food of the animals there is great plenty of moss, and for mankind an infinite variety of berries, of fish, and wild fruits.

The learned traveller and philosopher, Pallas,

tells us of various skeletons, bones, and teeth of elephants, or other immense animals, which have been found some fathoms deep in the earth of those inhospitable wilds which are covered with almost interminable snow. They are called mammoth's bones, and many specimens of them are to be seen in the museum of the academy of sciences at St. Petersburgh. As the constitution of the elephant does not appear suited to a rude atmosphere, these phenomena are amongst the important proofs of diluvian or some other great revolutions in nature. "Did these animals go thither while alive? What inducement led them? Have they been wafted thither after death? What a flood must it have been that carried them! or are they bones of sea animals?" *

The natives of all the northern and central districts are excessively hardy, but still it is no unusual thing for men to be frozen, so as either to die on the spot, or, without speedy assistance, for the limbs that are caught by the frost to fall off by degrees.

Nevertheless, the people are of robust health,

---

* Tooke.

long-lived, subject to few chronic diseases, and any slight colds they may take or obstructions of the pores are soon remedied by the hot rooms in which they are accustomed to sleep, and still more by the frequent use of their universally-beloved hot or vapour baths.

But the frigidity of the climate is far from being considered a calamity by the Russians. The frost, and the quantity of snow in connection with it, is, in one respect, of infinite advantage to the empire, as by that means the land-carriage is inconceivably facilitated. No sooner is the sledge-way formed, than all the country roads are covered with carriages. In several districts, masts, balks, fire-wood, &c., can only be fetched in the winter, especially from marshy forests. What immense quantities of flax, hemp, tobacco, deals, tallow, &c., are brought by sledge-way from the different provinces of Russia to the ports of the Baltic!

In short, the ice and the cold, though not without their disadvantages, are still of service in various ways. They also promote the pleasure of the inhabitants, by affording opportunity for the diversion of sledge and horse racing, and for that of the ice-hills, so much admired by the populace. The weight of these ice-hills, together with that of a multitude sometimes of five or six thousand persons standing about them on holidays, gives the spectator a surprising idea of the strength and solidity of the ice. It is usually about two feet thick on the Neva.

What may be executed in ice was shewn by the ice palace which the empress Anne caused to be built on the banks of the Neva in 1740. It was constructed, we are told, of huge quadrates of ice, hewn in the manner of free-stone. The edifice was fifty-two feet in length, sixteen in breadth, and twenty in height. The walls were three feet thick. In the several apartments were tables, chairs, beds, and all kinds of household furniture of ice. In front of the palace, besides pyramids and statues, stood six cannons, carrying balls of six pounds weight, and mortars of ice. From one of the former, as a trial, an iron ball, with only a pound of powder, was fired off. The ball went through a two-inch board, at sixty paces from the mouth of the cannon; and the piece of artillery, with its lavette, remained uninjured by the explosion. The illumination of the ice palace at night had an astonishingly grand effect.

This, however, is but a mimic artillery. But the ice may be spoken of in a more positive sense, as occasionally a most formidable rampart for the national defence against foreign invasion. Of this, the ruin which attended the armies of Charles XII. of Sweden, in 1709, and of the emperor Napoleon in 1812, were terrible instances. Almost similar sufferings from cold awaited an army of one of the renowned Mogul conquerors, some ages back, during an invasion of China.

On the breaking up of the ice at Petersburgh, which happens generally in April, it is formally announced by the firing of a certain number of cannon from the fortress, and by certain processions of the city authorities. Previous to these ceremonies no boat may navigate the Neva.

In the ninth century Novgorod was the capital. Some twenty years later, the victorious regent Oleg transferred the government to Kief in the south, which he had just conquered: Kief then enjoyed some portion of the Greek civilization. In the twelfth century, on account of the attacks of the Poles, and from other reasons, Vladimir, being more central, was chosen as the capital. In the fourteenth century, Moscow was deemed a still more eligible situation; and in 1703, in consideration of the maritime advantages of the site, and for the better securing of the then recent conquests from Sweden, the present splendid capital city of St. Petersburgh was founded, at an incredible expense of life and money.

This was the fifth change in the place of residence of the Russian Sovereigns; and there are many who think that they will again remove, if circumstances admit, to the more genial and inviting climes of the south.

From the middle of the ninth century to the middle of the eleventh century, or about 200 years,—being from the reign of the Norman chief, RURIC the Great, the founder of the Russian monarchy (if it may be so termed), to the decease of *Yœroslof* the Legislator in 1054, may be regarded as a period in its annals for the most part of prosperity and conquest.

Traditionary and other popular accounts agree that towards the beginning of the just mentioned period (the 9th century), Novgorod in the north, and Kief in the south of Russia, were wealthy and populous cities, carrying on a considerable commerce between Europe and Asia, being respectively the capitals of a large territory, and ruled by a republican or democratical form of government.

Anterior to that period, which is now about a thousand years ago, there are no traces or facts in story of the Russian people sufficiently ascertained to deserve remark for any useful purpose. And, as to their origin, it is totally lost in the "night of antiquity," and the researches of the learned have cast over it but a very feeble and dubious light.

The two or three following remarks, therefore, in relation to this point, can at best be only matter for curiosity or speculation. Fins, Huns, Slavonians, Scythians, and Goths, there is every reason to presume were amongst the earlier inhabitants of some of the countries now called Russia; and these, or the immediately adjoining regions, we may equally conclude, were the cradle of those countless swarms of barbarians which so often assailed the Greek and Roman empires during the first ages of Christianity; and which eventually overran, subdued, or colonized, half Europe and Asia.

The following is a summary of this hasty notice:

In the fifth century of the Christian era it is affirmed, that two hordes of a people called Slavonians, from the banks of the Danube (the country which it is thought Russia now in turn meditates appropriating) migrated towards the north, and built the towns of Kief and Novgorod; but even all this is involved in considerable uncertainty.

In 860, a body of the piratical nation, called Danes or Saxons,—Swedes, Scandinavians, or Goths, (the learned are not very unanimous as to which of these appellations they should be classed under,) were called in as allies, by the Novgorodians, during some violent intestine dissensions. As is not unusual in such cases, the allies soon became masters.

It was successive inroaders of the same people, also introduced most commonly during domestic troubles, who, in those ages, ravaged, laid waste, and ultimately subdued England. Ruric, as before mentioned, was the leader of that party of them which selected Russia as the theatre of their enterprises. He built, and surrounded with ramparts, the city of old Ladoga, not very far from the site of the modern St. Petersburgh. Subsequently, the victorious Ruric took possession of Novgorod, and selected it as the seat of his power.

From that period their authentic history as a nation begins.

Until the accession of *Peter*, which took place now about a hundred and forty years ago, they were, however, but little known or thought of in Europe.

Both they and their great Dukès, or Czars (for they had yet no Emperors), occasioned about as much interest in France, England, or Italy, as the affairs of the Shah of Persia do at present.

Peter's suppression of the Strelitz (the Janissaries of Muscovy), his combats with the Greek priesthood (who were almost as powerful as the Moollas are still in Turkey), his travels, his victory of Pultowa, soon attracted abundance of attention. Perhaps the impress of his genius, and that of his great successor Catherine, may be considered, at this day, as scarcely less vivid than during their life-time. The plans and the armies, whose impetus and formation are, in chief part, attributable to these sovereigns, are now casting lengthened and gloomy shadows over previously superior states.

APPENDIX.

No. I.

Proofs and Authorities referred to in the Text relative to the Supplies, means of Transport, and nature of the Country generally, along the Military Route treated of.

"BEING sent to purchase horses at a fair at Cossipoor, he (Mr. Moorcroft, the superintendent of the Company's stud in Bengal) discovered that the *great mart of this noble animal was at Bokhara,* and conceiving that it might be of infinite service to the army in India if a direct communication could be opened with the original breeders, he engaged a Brahmin to accompany him," &c. &c. ("Having reached the table-land of Tartary,") "he met with WHOLE DROVES OF HORSES, which he might have purchased at sixty rupees (about 7*l.* sterling) a-head." And again, "He saw behind the mountains great numbers of wild horses, and the Ghurk-hur, or wild ass: BUT HORSES SEEMED THE STAPLE COMMODITY OF THE COUNTRY. Tartary appears to be, in fact, the indigenous country of the horse. From Pegu to the CASPIAN, over all that extensive region which sweeps to the northward of the Himmaleh and the Hindoo Coosh, the horse is the most thriving animal, improving in size, strength, and beauty, as we proceed to the westward. In all this vast tract he is everywhere the companion of man—he shares with him his food, his tent, and his clothing."—*Quarterly Review*, No. 27.

"They breed sheep (the people of the province of Balk), camels, and *horses; and so numerous are the latter*, that there is scarcely a man in Toorkistaun so indigent as to walk on foot: even beggars travel on horseback, or at least upon camels and asses. As might be expected, the Usbeks produce swarms of light cavalry."—*Elphinstone*, p. 471.

"The spirit and beauty of the Tartarian horses have been long celebrated. The stud of a Noble Mogul sometimes contains 3000 or 4000 of these animals."—*Encyclopedia Britannica*, vol. xviii.

"The principal gardens are always on the outside of the castle; and THE FLOCKS AND HERDS OF HORSES OR CAMELS, which belong to the Khauns, are kept at distant pastures, and attended by servants who live in tents."—*Elphinstone*, p. 408.

"The horse trade (says Mr. Elphinstone, pp. 296, 297) requires a few words, from its importance. A great number of horses are annually sold in the north of India, under the name of Caubul horses; and in the west, under that of Candahar horses; but almost the whole of these come from Toorkistaun. No horses are bred at Caubul, except by men of property, for their own use; nor are the horses bred about Candahar exported. Some of the fine horses of the neighbourhood of Heraut are carried to other countries, but few or none to India. A good many horses are exported from Beloochistaun, as are some of the fine breed found on both sides of the Indus, to the north of the Salt range. But by far the greatest breeding country in the Caubul dominions is BALK; and it is from that province, and the Toorkmun country, lower down the Oxus (*Bokhara, Khiva*, &c.), that the bulk of those exported are brought. There are two sorts of horses most dealt in: one, rather small, but very stout, capable of much work, and cheap; the other, much larger, and more valued on that account, though not near so serviceable, except for war, where, owing to the Asiatic mode of fighting, size is of importance. The former, though of three sorts, are generally comprehended in the name of Toorkee or Usbekee, and are bred in Balk, and the provinces NEAR BOKHARA. The other is called Toorkemunee, and is really bred by the Toorkmuns *on both banks of the lower* OXUS. The great marts are Balk and Bokhara. Horses sell there at from *5l.* to *20l.* for a Toorkee, and from *20l.* to *100l.* for a Toorkmunee. The merchants generally buy them cheap and in bad order, and fatten them in the pasture of Caubul. The most famous place is the Nirkh Merdaun, west of Caubul, where a horse in the most emaciated state can be brought into condition in forty days, at an expense of five or six shillings. They first soil them with trefoil, and then give them lucerne. Many horses are sold in the country, and great numbers used to be sent on to India. The internal trade is increasing; many of the farmers (of Caubul) buying horses now, that formerly never thought of doing so; but the exportation to India has greatly fallen off. Wherever the British dominion extends, large armies of horse are changed for small ones of infantry; and there the gentlemen prefer Arabs. The native armies also have diminished, as the circle of their depredations has been circumscribed; and if the company's breeding studs are successful, the horse trade between India and Toorkistaun will be annihilated."

"LA KHIVIE (says Mouravief, pp. 329, 334, 335) est également riche en bétail; on y rencontre de grands troupeaux de chameaux, de moutons et de bœufs. Ces animaux s'y contentent de pâturage fort maigres; l'on voit paitre des chameaux et des moutons dans des endroits où un européen n'imaginerait jamais qu'un animal quelquonque pût trouver à pâturer . . . . . . Cette ville (*Ourghendj*) est devenue le point central du commerce des KHIVIENS ; elle offre un aspect tres-vivant. Ses nombrenses boutiques remplies de marchandises de prix, venues de toutes les parties de l'orient, éblouissent la vue par leur eclat. Il regne dans ses rues un bruit continuel, occasionné par l'affluence des marchands et *les cris des chameaux, qui plient sur les pesant fardeaux dont il, sont chargés*. . . . . . . Les caravanes transporte sauspeine, aux moyen de leurs chameaux, des marchandises sur tous les points."

"A Tartar horse-race is well calculated to try the bottom of the animal. The Turcomans have no idea of a short heat; THEY ASSEMBLE A GREAT MULTITUDE OF HORSES, at a spot where they are to start, generally a good day's journey from the winning-post."—*Quarterly Review*, 1815.

"The caravans to Toorkistaun are all on horses or poneys, probably on account of the very mountainous roads, which lie in one part over the snowy ridge of Hindoo Coosh. Those which go to Chinese Toorkistaun, set off from Cashmeer and Peshawer: Caubul is the great mart of independent Toorkistaun. Candahar and Heraut, for Persia. The Indian trade is more divided; that of the Punjaub, and the north of Hindostan, comes to Peshawer."—*Elphinstone*.

"The further the mission advanced," observes M. Nazaroff, "through Turkistan, now a part of Khokand, the more fixed the population appeared; the tents of the Tartars were exchanged for houses of stone, and fields cultivated with grain, among which towns and villages interspersed, were seen on every side. Everything now wore the appearance of an improved civilization. . . . . The people of Khokand speak the

Turkish language with the greatest purity; and are far advanced (says M. Nazaroff) in civilization."

"The borders of this lake are the resort of various wandering tribes, who barter their horses, camels, and sheep, with the caravans, for clothing and other articles of necessity and luxury."

It was here, (the city of Khokand, the capital of Khokania,) in the centre of those interminable plains, where GENGHIS-KHAN was in the habit of assembling a general council of all the Khans, governors and military chiefs of his extensive empire; and where, we are told, were once assembled 500 ambassadors from the conquered countries only. It was here that the magnificent feast was given by TIMOUR, on the marriage of his six grandsons; where, according to *Gibbon*, following the statement of Sherefeddin, "the plain was spread with pyramids of meat, and vases of every kind of liquor, to which thousands of guests were courteously invited;" where "pearls and rubies were showered on the heads of the brides and bridegrooms, and contemptuously abandoned to their attendants;" where "a general indulgence was proclaimed, every law relaxed, every pleasure was allowed, the people was free, the sovereign was idle." But from this oriental style of describing the ancient state of those countries, we return to the mere matter of fact of the present time.

The Baron Meyendorf states, that *six thousand camels* are employed in the *foreign* trade of Bokhara; of which number, three thousand go every year to the frontiers of Russia, Orenburg, Troitz, &c. The few years that have elapsed, are said to have added largely to the above numbers.

The flat-bottomed boats used by the natives on the Sir are not of very good workmanship. Their construction is described by the officers of the Russian embassy. Most of them, it appears, are so large, that from four to six camels can be carried over at once; and for every camel, they charge seventeen ells of a coarse Bucharian cotton stuff: they will not take money. The price was considered to be high, but the labour is said to have been considerable . . . . The inhabitants of the islands of the Aral possess a very considerable number of large vessels, and live *entirely* by fishing.

The boats employed on the Oxus, or Amou, are much larger and better constructed than those on the Sir; so much so, that they are capable of containing fifty horses. They have a large sail and rudder, and are towed by horses when ascending the stream. The usual passage of these boats laden with merchandise, proceeding from Khiva to near Bokhara, is seven days. The Oxus is navigable the whole way from its mouth to within two marches of Balk. From Balk to Attock is (according to Mr. Fraser's account) under five hundred miles. One of the great stations on this line would be the city of Peshawer, situated in a highly cultivated and abundant plain. It is fifty miles west of Attock. Towards the end of the winter of 1809, Shah Shaja and his army *forded* the *Indus*, at a place above Attock.

" Their favourite food (the Usbecks) is horse-flesh, and mare's-milk made into kimmir: they drink tea boiled with milk, and oil made from the fat tails of the Doombeh sheep. They live partly in tents, and partly in houses, resembling those of the Afghauns. IN BOKHARA, *and the tract of country* BETWEEN THAT AND THE CASPIAN SEA, the greater part of the people reside in tents, and follow pasturage; *their stock consists of sheep, camels*, AND HORSES; THE LATTER ARE SO COMMON AND SO NUMEROUS, THAT EVERY TUR-

"COMAN HAS HIS HORSE, *and even beggars travel on horseback.*"—*Quarterly Review,** No. xxvii., p. 187.

No. II.

"FROM the nature of the country, the charms of which were heightened by novelty, and by the expectations we formed of the sights and incidents which we should meet with among so wild and extraordinary a people, it may be supposed that these morning expeditions were pleasing and interesting. Our evening rides were not less delightful, when we went out among the gardens round the city, and admired the richness and repose of the landscape, contrasted with the gloomy magnificence of the surrounding mountains, which were often involved in clouds and tempests, while we enjoyed the quiet and sunshine of the plain. The gardens are usually embellished with buildings, among which the cupolas of Mahometan tombs make a conspicuous figure." *Caubul.*

Speaking of a previous day's march through a mountain-district, the people of which are notorious for

---

* A more recent writer, however, in the same work, differs entirely from his predecessor.

"He farther states, 'that the property of the country consists in cattle, camels, and horses; that the latter are in droves of thousands together;' this, we shall content ourselves by observing, is physically impossible. *Where the Colonel has discovered 'that the deserts* (that of Kirghis being one of them), *in geographical maps, by no means invariably infer sterility,'* we are at a loss to find out, and all the information that we possess (!) entirely negatives the assertion, that 'the means of transport are here more abundant than in any part of the world'!"—*Quarterly, January last.*

their marauding and predatory habits—" By this time we had approached a little ruined tower in the mouth of the valley, and discovered a great many armed Kheiberees, sitting on the hills, looking wistfully at the camels passing. The chiefs only came to us, and asked for a present. It gave me a strange notion of the system of manners in Caubul, that these avowed robbers should come up and ask for a present; and that Moosa Khaun, in his rich dress and golden arms, should sit almost unattended in the midst of their matchlocks, and refuse them." (Moosa Khaun was a Dooraunee nobleman, appointed to attend on, and conduct the embassy to court.)

Right Bank of the Indus. " We passed (the Indus) in good flat-bottomed boats, made of fir, and *capable of carrying from thirty to forty tons.* Our camels had their feet tied, and were thrown into the boats like any other baggage: our horses also crossed in boats. The elephants alone swam, to the great astonishment of the people of the country,* who, probably, had never seen an animal of the kind before .... The cultivation was flourishing, but not extensive, though water is abundant; and the soil, to appearance, enjoys all that richness and fecundity for which inundated countries are so famous."—*Elphinstone.*

---

* " The notions entertained of us by the people (near the Indus) were not a little extraordinary. They believed we carried great guns, packed up in trunks; and that we had certain small boxes, so contrived as to explode, and kill half a dozen men each, without hurting us. Some thought we could raise the dead; and there was a story current, that we had made and animated a wooden ram, at Mooltaun; that we had sold him as a ram; and that it was not till the purchaser began to eat him, that the material of which he was made was discovered."

No. III.

The Expedition of Bekewitz to Khiva, by order of Peter the Great.

ALEXANDER BEKEWITZ, son of a Circassian prince,* captain of the Czar's body-guard, acquainted with the Tartar language, had a body of three thousand men placed under his command, to proceed to the pretended mouths of the Kizil-daria, and to take possession of the adjacent countries. The Tartars, uneasy to see the Russians making so many visits to this place, had, *it was said*, turned aside the course of the river, by damming it up with a strong dyke, and conducting the water, in three canals, to the lake Aral. Bekewitz arrived with his army, and searched in vain for the river by which he hoped to ascend to Khiva. The khaun met him with a numerous army, but was soon defeated by means of the European artillery. Mortified and rendered desperate by this defeat, the khaun sent to inquire of the Russian general what were the complaints of Russia, and what sacrifices were required of him. Bekewitz, full of the notion of the artificial change of direction which had been given to the Kizil-daria, demands of the khaun that he should open the dykes which prevented the river from running into the Caspian Sea, and thus restore it to its old course. The Tartar prince replied that this operation was beyond his power, and that it was impossible to close up the channels in which the river followed its new direction. Bekewitz then proposed to execute the project with his own men, provided their safety were ensured by the delivery of hostages To this proposal the Tartars willingly agreed, and the hostages were given. These, at the same time, acted as guides to the Russian army,

* *Malte-Brun.*

which marched five days towards the supposed dry bed of the river. In every quarter they met with nothing but small puddles of stagnant water. The soldiers were exhausted with thirst. The guides, with the most perfidious intentions, proposed to the Russians that they should divide themselves into small parties, and go in different directions. The Russian commander was weak enough to follow the advice of his enemies. The small Russian army was no sooner dispersed in these unknown tracts, than the Tartars, who had watched them, attacked their feeble detachments on all sides. Some were put to the sword, and the rest reduced to slavery. The unfortunate Bekewitz was taken into the presence of the khaun, and hacked to pieces. His skin was dried, and made into the cover of a drum, which was preserved at Khiva as a trophy, to testify to posterity the disastrous issue of an expedition so ignorantly planned, and conducted with so little prudence.

No. IV.

Observations on our future Intercourse with China.

VARIOUS are the instances on record of plans suggested by men whose enterprise or sagacity preceded their age, not adopted or succeeded in at the time, but nevertheless coming eventually into operation, after, perhaps, a long interval—an infallible proof of the original conformity of those plans with sound principles. Of this description may be classed, perhaps, some of those of the Czar Peter of Russia, now realising themselves.

The first Lord Clive proposed, I believe, some sixty

or seventy years ago, to undertake an attack upon China with 10,000 men*. Some twenty or thirty years hence, *if we still remain in secure possession of India*, circumstances may possibly bring about a reconsideration of that plan, although, perhaps, not so much, in the first instance, with a view to conquest, as for the purpose of compelling a free and unlimited commercial intercourse with the vast empire in question. In such case, the population in the East, brought to administer by their purchases to the commerce and maritime power of Britain, might become two or three fold more numerous than they now are; and in this manner would be provided a new outlet, and pregnant source of reviving activity and relief both for the merchant and artisan. And here it may be observed, that that branch of our external trade which is carried on with Asia is unequivocally the most promising; since, so far from depression, it has been advancing rapidly.

Thus are there increased motives (the retention of the present and the realization of the future) for guarding with vigilant foresight, and extending, if practicable, our positions, both territorial and maritime, in that quarter. If at any time our power on shore shall be restricted or seriously disputed, it is obvious that a naval force alone, on seas so remote from England, could afford but a precarious protection. A sum, equal to that expended on discourteously-received embassies—a tithe of what was incurred in the prosecution of the arduous Burmese war, so frivolous in origin and doubtful in expediency, would, probably, go far to defraying the charge of effectually intimidating, and thereby, on commercial points, reducing to the utmost complaisance, the Mantchoo rulers. The

* It is the same number of troops which some Russian writers have speculated upon for the same purpose.

grandeur of the consequences of an undertaking should not be regarded as the measure of its difficulty.

The western Tartarian provinces, in which so many rebellions occur, and where, according to the Pekin journals, such numerous and valiant armies are kept on foot, may, perhaps, at some future period, feel the influence of the Russian arms.

But the vast mass of the people and property of China are to be found along the one chief internal communication—the "Great Imperial Canal *"—1660 miles long, and which may mainly be considered as belonging to the *sea-board;* and, therefore, so far as we are concerned, offering peculiar advantages of access.

In China, there are two people—the conquerors and the conquered; the former, as so frequently occurs, being the least numerous, but both being now about equally effeminate. The former are of the same race which reigned at Delhi; and it is even the same family which governs, the imperial pageant of another branch of which is still tolerated under our power in Hindostan.

But many assert, that the least resort to coercion with the Chinese would be the instant destruction of the tea-trade;—that the first cannon-shot would be the signal for a mandate to the Hong merchants, interdicting us thenceforth from purchasing this their staple produce. But though, as we are told, of a cramped and puerile intellect, they are an abundantly money-loving people; and though their cunning may prompt them to threaten, it would probably go hard with them, before resorting to any measure of this kind. The financial injury would be theirs, the inconvenience or withdrawal of a luxury ours. At all events, the remedy would be an easy one.

---

* Ellis. Klaproth. Barrow.

The black tea is grown in the province of Fokein; the green, in that of Kiangnan. The former is carried on the backs of porters over a chain of mountains* interposing between Fokein and Canton; and the nearest place of its growth to the latter port of embarkation is upwards of five hundred miles. The green, again, is cultivated at a distance of seven or eight hundred miles; but there is for its conveyance partly an inland navigation. The mode of conveyance, in both cases, must considerably enhance the price. It so happens that both Fokein and Kiangnan are maritime provinces. And there is little doubt that if, at any future time, it should be resolved on to place a small British force in the occupation of a port or two on the shores of those provinces, a Chinese army (by concurrent accounts, a very burlesque assemblage) could not find it very easy to dislodge us. And thus, by this simple process, might the tea henceforth be obtained, at *first cost*, from the actual cultivators of the shrub, whose shrewdness would not be long in discovering the superior advantage of taking our silver, or even our Manchester or Birmingham goods, in preference to dealing with us in a more hostile way†.

The porter carriage alone of the black tea over the mountains is estimated to cost 150,000*l*. per annum. This the British consumer of the beverage at present pays. The saving in this item alone (which is only a small part of the extra price for land conveyance at present paid by us) is the interest of a larger sum than

---

* *Whitmore. Staunton. Timkowski.*

† A curious fact is mentioned by Mr. Whitmore in his speech of last session—that of the Russians selling some British stuffs at Kiakta to the Chinese for 8*s*. a yard, which an English trader could afford to sell on the sea-coast of China at 2*s*. 6*d*.

would be necessary for an operation on the limited scale alluded to; and of which the chief consequence, as an inducement, would of course be the prodigious field it might yield for commercial enterprise. We already return to the Hindoos the cotton of their own rearing in a manufactured state, cheaper and better than they could make it, else they would not buy it; and this, notwithstanding the additional cost of sea-carriage of about twenty-four thousand miles. Let any one calculate the profit on a similar facility of supplying a people double in numbers, and, perhaps, quadruple at least in the degree of their resources.*

The military and political helplessness of this empire has been long a topic of notoriety. The maritime or eastern part of it, which is the heart of its means, is altogether, and as yet exclusively, at our mercy. Pretenders to royalty are constantly rising up in the distant provinces. A serious rebellion is now waging; and a small efficient European force, of any kind, passed in to the support of any of the numerous insurgent forces so often assembling to the *westward*, might have a widely influential effect. Some fifty years hence, perhaps, some such interference may come within the scope of Russian ambition.

Some persons have supposed that the seeming union and implicit obedience manifested by the Chinese, in general, towards their superiors, and in conforming to established institutions, would impart a power of resistance in case of attack; but a closer inspection will not, it is thought, bear out this anticipation. Fear, not love, is their bond of union. It is the whip of the Tartar, conjoined with the native paternal rod previ-

* "The taste for British goods has been introduced, and seems now pretty well established. The superior quality of our cloths seems to be very generally felt and acknowledged."—*Staunton.*

ously in use, by which the mass is as yet restrained and kept together; in the continuance of which, no doubt, the mental decrepitude to which they are reduced by their strange laws is a powerful auxiliary.

The mandarins are stated to be far from being what Voltaire represented them—philosophers, occupied with contemplations on the beauties of natural religion, who, raised above human passions, watch with fatherly care over the frailer virtue of their brethren. They are not a set of patriots, who guard with integrity, and defend with energy, the sacred trust of public justice; they are nothing else but the satellites of an absolute despot. No disunion, it is true, may be perceivable amongst the aristocracy, because, while they hold the rod over the heads of the multitude, they see the imperial lash waving over their own. The despotism of the Mantchoo sovereigns keeps that of the grandees in order, and obliges them to remain united. There is no effectual resistance, therefore, in the eastern districts, although many revolts. The people are without courage, though possessed of so much chicanery and finesse. They find it, in short, safer to preserve a part of their precious property by grovelling at the feet of their masters, than to risk the loss of the whole in order to obtain a relaxation of their bonds and a remedy for exaction. From such a people, a prudent invader could have but little occasion to fear.

But in fact, on a subject of commerce, if we should exhibit force, but at the same time manage to avoid materially compromising the dignity of the empire, it is contrary to reason to suppose that the Chinese government would seriously quarrel with us; for the trade of Canton, without reference to an extension of it, not only produces a great circulation of money in most of the provinces, but also procures the emperor and his ministers a considerable and certain revenue.

The Russians even admit*, that England is much more favourably situated with respect to China, than the empire of the Czars. Our conquests in India, though the court of Pekin pretends to know nothing of them, must necessarily excite some reflections in the Celestial Empire. It has, probably, no inclination to measure its strength with the nation which reigns on the seas, and whose standards are now even within view of the imperial confines. No remonstrance was ventured on, when we chastised the Nepaulese, and dismembered their territory. The Celestial cabinet deemed it the more prudent course to feign ignorance.

Sir George Staunton dwells, in a recent publication, on the excessive jealousy created (though unavowed) by the knowledge of our entire conquest of Hindostan, and, latterly, of a tributary to China (Nepaul); and also on the terror caused by the occasional appearance of some British cruisers along the Chinese shores. He indulges in expressions of astonishment and gratification at the unexpected "*placability and forbearance*" with which the Chinese bore with the "forcible occupation and retention of Macao by a British force (a mere detachment!) during the last three months of the year 1808, *in absolute defiance of all the local forces and authorities*, Chinese as well as Portuguese." When this unhappy interruption ceased, they, on the first moment (he says) that it was announced, allowed the trade to recommence and fall into its ordinary channels. Again, in another place, Sir George lauds with warmth the increased kindness towards us, and the growing disposition to relax their prohibitive vexations in our favour. He cannot sufficiently *admire the wisdom or the good fortune by which we have been hitherto extricated* from the numberless difficulties with which the trade with

---

* See Timkowski's Embassy to Pekin, 1820.

Canton is in his opinion surrounded. It never once occurs to the learned and highly estimable Baronet, how brief an explanation (and, perhaps, quite as correct a one) may be given of this new and wonderful "placability"—viz. fondness for our dollars, increasing fears of our cannon; reluctance to forego the one, awakened conviction of inability to meet the other!

The following is a remark, bearing on the same point, from the pen of the eminent orientalist, Klaproth. It is in referring to the refusal of the court of Pekin to permit the further progress to the capital of the Great Russian Embassy of 1805:—"Had Count Golofkin come at the head of an army, he would probably have succeeded better than being merely loaded with compliments and presents, which the Chinese choose to call tribute."

May not the same commentary apply to the failure of Lord Amherst's embassy?

Finally, all that is meant by this train of observation is only this—that there are probably prospective, as well as present interests, of a vast and yet uncalculated value, involved in the safety and consolidation of our Eastern possessions; forming, as they do, the base of our influence, power, and commerce in that quarter of the world.

No. V.

Legal opinion on the Blockade of the Dardanelles.

THE following, from a private letter, may be regarded in the light of a law opinion, being that of a distinguished member (Dr. Edwards) of the Court of Admiralty :—

"The blockade of the Dardanelles is the most daring outrage upon neutral rights that ever was committed. It is not a blockade of Constantinople, but a blockade of entire seas—of countless miles of coast both in Europe and Asia, and actually shuts us out from some *Russian* ports. We may not have much to do in those ports, but the violation of principle is the same.—Mr. . . . . . talks about the belligerent rights of Russia, without seeming to know that the blockade of Constantinople alone would not be a legitimate exercise of that right, unless Constantinople was *actually invested.* True it is that, last war, we declared the entire coasts and ports of the enemy in a state of blockade, but that was never pretended to be the result of any recognized belligerent right. Sir W. Scott was always most anxious to explain that it was a departure from the general rule, and only to be justified as a retaliatory measure in consequence of Buonaparte having placed all the ports of England under interdict by his Berlin and Milan decrees. Our language to neutrals was—'If you are not strong enough to compel him to revoke these decrees, which violate the law of nations to your injury and ours, we, who are struggling for our very existence as a nation, must try whether we cannot bring him to reason, by retaliating upon him his own violent measures.' This peculiar and anomalous case does not apply in the present instance, and we must return to the old doctrine, that we have a right, as neutrals, to send to the ports of either of the belligerents whatever we have to sell, except munitions of war, unless any particular port shall happen to be in a state of actual siege."

NOTE.

I THINK my acknowledgments are due to a writer in an able and much-esteemed periodical work, for the notice with which he has honoured the Essay, before mentioned, on the affairs of Russia. The remarks in this critique are, in general, so apposite, that I can scarcely refrain from giving some of them. The following is the termination or climax of the article:—

"We are just in time," says the well-informed writer, "to state the *disastrous finale*, which we have received from an *authentic source*, of the rash and precipitous invasion of the Turkish territory by Russia—that alarming invasion which, in the opinion of Lieut.-Col. Evans, demanded an immediate armed intervention of all the powers of Europe, to stay the overwhelming career of the autocrat, who aimed at little less than universal dominion. The Turks, however, have done it effectually of themselves, single-handed, without the assistance of any one power, European or Asiatic; and the Sublime Sultan may now boast, with the Roman warrior,—

> .... 'like an eagle in a dove-cote, I
> Flutter'd your *Russians* in *Bulgaria;*
> *Alone* I did it.'

Fluttered, indeed, with a vengeance! *The rout was complete; resembling, on a smaller scale, that of the French from Moscow. We are told that not a living creature escaped out of this horrible Bulgaria, save man—and he, bare and destitute of every thing that constitutes a soldier—without arms, without accoutrements, without baggage, and, as the French would say, completely demoralized;* all the draught horses, and cattle of every kind; all those of the cavalry and artillery dead;—all the guns, carriages, waggons, ammunition, and provisions, left behind as spoil for the Turks. The extent of these disasters is endeavoured to be concealed at Petersburg, *where the war, from the first, was unpopular;* but now men shake their heads, by which, like the shake of Burleigh's in the play, they mean a great deal, though they say nothing; and they are afraid to write, as all letters are inspected at the post-office. It is to be hoped that this disastrous campaign will have taught the young emperor a lesson of moderation, which will counsel him to seek for peace rather than conquest."

This, I dare say, is sublime; very poetical; and, certainly, no less *prophetic* of subsequent events.

I rather apprehend, however, that there may be here some trivial error as to the mere matter of fact of the Russian army, to a man, having evacuated or perished in Bulgaria; inasmuch as it appears (by the accounts of the belligerents themselves) that not only the garrison of Varna, but some fifteen or twenty thousand more of these exterminated troops, remained in the advanced position of Paravadi, covering, throughout the year, a large portion of the pashalick of Bulgaria;—an unsuccessful attempt upon this same Paravadi, about the beginning of the month of June last, by the army of the Grand Vizier, having been attended with very inconvenient consequences to that commander's army.

I confess I was a little startled in reading the following passage:—

"Leave we, then, the west to take care of itself, and say a few words on the too oft repeated and hackneyed topics—a Russian invasion of India, and the destruction of our India and China trade, by diverting it into a new channel overland. On these subjects, which, since the days of the Czar Peter, have become, as we have elsewhere observed, a sort of periodical nervous intermittent, Colonel Evans appears to us to be completely floating adrift, without sail or compass. With regard to the first point—*the army destined for the invasion of India is supposed to assemble at Orenburg, march for Attock by Herat,*" &c., &c.—p. 35.

He then goes on to shew that it would be quite impossible for an army to march to Herat, Bokhara, &c.; being one thousand miles across the steppes, or deserts, on either bank of the *Sir* river, the Kesil Koum, &c.

But, by referring to p. 40, it will be seen that this idea of a march of a thousand miles, through the Khirgis steppes and crossing the SIR river, is entirely the fruit of the imagination of the reviewer. He has mistaken, it would appear, the *Oxus* for the *Sir;* and a progress chiefly by water, for one by land.

Again—" He goes on to state that a *considerable* commerce *is carried on between Orenburg and Khiva, Samarcand, &c.—a position which we are obliged to deny, and to state distinctly that* no *commerce is carried on by Russia with these countries; its* only *Asiatic commerce being with China, at Kiakta, to the value of about five millions of roubles.*" For which statement, the authority named is *Weydemer's Tableaux Statistiques.*

By the following, from *Weydemer*, the reader will see with what scrupulous fidelity this second '*Daniel*' of a critic makes use of the names of writers. Only about forty millions (see note) is the mistake made in this item.

RUSSIAN COMMERCE WITH ASIA.

	Ships.	Exportation.	Importation.
Mer Caspienne......	432....	7,810,925....	834,024 rbls.
Frontière sur terre depuis la mer Caspienne jusqu'à Semipolatinsk	,, ...	4,216,817....	6,267,298
Commerce de Kiakhta	,, ...	5,503,344....	5,503,344
Georgie	,, ...	890,498....	3,809,158
TOTAL....		13,193,146	19,389,158 rbls.
			13,193,146
			32,582,304 rbls.*

(13th *Tableau Statistique de Weydemer*.)

The Bishop of Calcutta, the late Dr. James, is then quoted, in proof of the inefficiency of the Russian army in numbers, discipline, and bravery.—"*The truth is, the accounts of the Russian army, of its discipline and valour, have been grossly exaggerated.*"

An ingenious "CRITICAL HISTORIAN," of some celebrity, candidly acknowledges in his preface, that though he never was in India, he is fortunately more competent to acquire a knowledge of it in one year, without stirring from his closet, than any other man, civil, mili-

* If to this we add, suppose, one-third of the export and import estimate for the Euxine and Azof seas, as a probable proportion of it carried on with Asiatic ports, we shall have another sum of about eleven millions. Total export (25,885,171) and import (8,448,025) evaluation for the commerce of the Euxine and Azof—34,323,196 roubles. Conveyed in 1497 merchant-ships. But if one may rely on Mr. Whitmore, who is, I believe, well informed on such points, the value of goods now sent from Russia to *Kiakta alone*, has risen to twenty-five millions roubles (1,000,000*l.* sterling), and the consumption of tea in Russia to 25,000,000 lbs.

tary, or political, might do, during a whole life of personal experience in that country! It is no doubt in the same way that the bishop, the civilian critic, and the Anglo-Russian merchants, who have sent forth their "*Few words on our relations with Russia*," have acquired their very superior knowledge of the efficiency of armies and military tactics generally.

Only one other little mistake (out of an uninterrupted series of them) I shall advert to.

The learned critic is quite satisfied of the absurdity of supposing that a Russian force could march from the Caspian to Khiva; he is equally satisfied, that there are neither means of transport nor provisions to be had for troops at Khiva or at Bokhara. "The Oasis of Khiva (he says) is another of the '*three earthly paradises*' of the Arabian writers; but it is a small one, and might, perhaps, *furnish a breakfast* for a Russian army, *but heaven only knows where they would get a dinner*."

In short, the advance of the Russian frontier in the direction of India is, he informs us, totally chimerical; and *Colonels Mouravief* and *Meyendorf* are the names mentioned as authorities for this assertion (!)—the very individuals who so strenuously represent to their government the facility and advantage of the measure!!!

It appears, from some pamphlets it gave rise to, that the author of this *amusing* article on a *serious* subject is a distinguished literary and official character, remarkable for the very creditable zeal with which he has patronized geographical science. I am afraid, however, that when he took this subject of Russia in hand, his attention may have been a little too much diverted—perhaps by some knotty point concerning the *North Pole* or the *Source of the Niger*. It certainly requires not only considerable abilities, but also a lucky system of guessing, to review a work with success, and quote the titles of others,—without having had leisure to look over their contents.

And this reminds one of the story of the Greek philosopher, who wrote a book to prove,—that a person might not know the less of a subject by having read something upon it.

Note omitted at page 45.

"They (the Persians) know nothing of the modern science of war, being entirely ignorant of the principles of fortification and of the arts of attack and defence. . . . . . Another great defect in the organization of the armies of this country is the total want of good officers. . . . . They (the commanders of the troops) are totally ignorant of the duties of their profession, and open to every kind of corruption and bribery. . . . Avarice is the leading feature in the Persian character; and, at the shrine of this detestable vice, every feeling of virtue and honour is sacrificed without a blush."—*Kinneir's Memoir*, p. 35.

FINIS.